The Praxis

A Transcendent Theology of the Spiritual and Temporal

In association with Zero State Media, Project ZSM011

© Dirk C Bruere 2011

All rights reserved. No part of this book may be reproduced, transmitted in any form or by any means, electronic or mechanical, including photocopying, recording or by any information storage or retrieval system without permission in writing from the copyright holder.

Published by Dirk Bruere

22 Milburn Road
Bedford
England
MK41 0NZ

ISBN: 978-0-9567587-3-6

Savitri - Sri Aurobindo

I saw the Omnipotent's flaming pioneers
Over the heavenly verge which turns towards life
Come crowding down the amber stairs of birth;
Forerunners of a divine multitude,
Out of the paths of the morning star they came
Into the little room of mortal life.
I saw them cross the twilight of an age,
The sun-eyed children of a marvellous dawn,
The great creators with wide brows of calm,
The massive barrier-breakers of the world
And wrestlers with destiny in her lists of will,
The labourers in the quarries of the gods,
The messengers of the Incommunicable,
The architects of immortality.
Into the fallen human sphere they came,
Faces that wore the Immortal's glory still,
Voices that communed still with the thoughts of God,
Bodies made beautiful by the spirit's light,
Carrying the magic word, the mystic fire,
Carrying the Dionysian cup of joy,
Approaching eyes of a diviner man,
Lips chanting an unknown anthem of the soul,
Feet echoing in the corridors of Time.
High priests of wisdom, sweetness, might and bliss,
Discoverers of beauty's sunlit ways
And swimmers of Love's laughing fiery floods
And dancers within rapture's golden doors,
Their tread one day shall change the suffering earth
And justify the light on Nature's face.
Although Fate lingers in the high Beyond
And the work seems vain on which our heart's force was spent,
All shall be done for which our pain was borne.
Even as of old man came behind the beast
This high divine successor surely shall come
Behind man's inefficient mortal pace,
Behind his vain labour, sweat and blood and tears:
He shall know what mortal mind barely durst think,
He shall do what the heart of the mortal could not dare.
Inheritor of the toil of human time,
He shall take on him the burden of the gods;
All heavenly light shall visit the earth's thoughts,
The might of heaven shall fortify earthly hearts;
Earth's deeds shall touch the superhuman's height,
Earth's seeing widen into the infinite.

Acknowledgments

Special thanks to:

Amon Kalkin and Fiona MacKenzie

I believe like a child that suffering will be healed and made up for, that all the humiliating absurdity of human contradictions will vanish like a pitiful mirage, like the despicable fabrication of the impotent and infinitely small Euclidean mind of man, that in the world's finale, at the moment of eternal harmony, something so precious will come to pass that it will suffice for all hearts, for the comforting of all resentments, for the atonement of all the crimes of humanity, for all the blood that they've shed; that it will make it not only possible to forgive but to justify all that has happened. - Fyodor Dostoyevsky

Also thanks to the Sri Aurobindo Ashram Trust for the quotation from *Savitri*...
to Jamie Dunbaugh, for the quotation from his poem *The Death of Illusory Love and the Ascension of Being* ...
to Fiona MacKenzie and S MacKenzie for the cover art...
to Adrian Giddings for the logo above
Extract from *The Weight of Glory* by C S Lewis copyright © C.S. Lewis Pte. Ltd. 1949 – Extract reprinted by permission

Disclaimer

The accuracy and completeness of information provided herein and opinions stated herein are not guaranteed, nor are they warranted to produce any particular results. The advice, strategies and techniques contained herein may not be suitable for every individual. The author shall not be liable for any losses, injuries or fatalities incurred as a consequence of the use and application, directly or indirectly, of any information presented in this work. Neither does the author condone or encourage any activity described herein that may be illegal in any particular jurisdiction. Whilst I hope you find the contents of this book interesting and informative, the contents are for general information only.

Table of Contents

Acknowledgments 4

Read Me! 7
   Read Me! (Introduction) 7

Non-Dualism 13
   Non-Dualism 13
   Spirit 14
   Spirit As Inner Essence 14
   Spirit As Incorporeal Consciousness 16
   Soul 19
   On Being Spiritual 20

Eternal Life 23
   Eternal Life 23
   Who Are You? 26
   Immortality – Whether You Want It Or Not 27
   Dying, But Not Dead 29

The Great Work 31
   The Great Work 31
   The Gnostic Connection 33
   The Tree Of Life 35
   The Symbol Of Life 36
   The Transmutation Of Matter 38
   The Messiah 39
   The Apocalypse 43
   Resurrecting The Dead 46
   Transmigration Of Souls 47

Nature 49
   Nature 49
   The Bright Green Future 50
   The End Of Suffering 53
   Uplifting 55
   Mirror Mirror 56
   The PostHuman Condition 58

Dreams of Brahma 67
   Dreams Of Brahma 67

 From The Deep Past To Far Future...75
 Doomsday..79
 Theodicy...80
 Judgment Day...84
 Fate, Angels And Demons..87
 The Demonic Worlds..88

Ethics...91

 Ethics..91
 The Oath...91
 The Golden Rule...94
 Compassion..95

The Praxis..97

 The Praxis...97
 Immanentizing The Eschaton..98
 Organization Of The Praxis..98
 Sacraments...100
 Rites And Rituals..100
 Initiation Into A Domain Of The Praxis......................................102
 Formal Ceremonies And Meetings...104
 Birth And Naming..105
 Marriage..106
 Funeral Rites..108

The End..111

 The End...111

Read Me! (Introduction)

The beginning is a very delicate time. Know then that it is the year 2011CE, and this is your destiny

This work has largely sprung from several sources separated by decades. The first was a question asked as part of a written examination in the art of Shorinji Kempo - "What is religion?". The second is more subtle and flows from the simple idea of actually following very general scientific beliefs concerning the true nature of the world we live in to their logical conclusions, no matter how insane they may appear. The third is that of Transhumanism and its parallels to religion in general and Christianity in particular. Not to say that Transhumanism, latterly re-branded as HumanityPlus or "H+", is founded on anything but an explicitly materialist basis, but it does nevertheless address those questions that might once have been the sole province of religion – those of life, death, deity (of a sort), immortality, resurrection and the destiny of the universe. It is the apotheosis of materialism, yet eschews taking on the mantle of a modern faith. Its mainly male adherents tend to be atheists who generally ignore or disparage its religious implications and character. By dismissing out of hand spirituality (no matter how vaguely defined) it alienates a large percentage of the population.

I hope this work goes some way towards rectifying that situation, and also some way towards blunting its naive materialist message with a complementary and ancient spiritual one. Therefore, as a result, extending what is a life affirming and ultimately optimistic philosophy to those who have either never heard of it or have been repelled by the boisterous crudity of its youthful and somewhat hubristic exuberance. Whether Transhumanists like it or not, H+ is not only the most important philosophical movement in history but additionally the most important spiritual one. For reference, this can be considered a sequel to my previous book *Technomage*.

Returning to the first question, I now believe I am in a better position to answer it. Simply put, a religion needs to satisfy as many of these conditions as possible:

- It must provide a doctrine
- It must have canonical texts that expound upon that doctrine
- It must offer an ethical framework
- It must offer an explanation of the world around us and the world within
- It must offer hope and comfort in adversity
- It must offer community, fellowship, mutual support and a better way to live
- It must empower the individual
- It must offer a mission in life beyond the mundane
- It must offer a vision of a life beyond this one
- It must offer transcendence

There are additionally other recipes for success in the modern world, most notably inclusiveness by race, gender, sexual orientation and nationality. Nobody should be excluded because of factors over which they have no control, nor be made second class citizens as is the case with women in the major monotheistic religions. Of course, some might have noted the omission of one factor quite important in the spread of the mainstream religions – coercion. However, the use of force in conversion is not something that any religion starts with, even if it becomes a major feature later. Nor, in our particular case, could it ever be justified. However, an explicit threat lodged in the memes of the major monotheistic religions is that failure to embrace them means death, or worse. In some ways this is true of the Praxis, because if we do not embrace at least some of its H+ aims billions will die who should not die and even more who have died will never live again. Anyway, moving on...

There are four philosophical pillars upon which this work is based. These are:

- Non Duality – that "reality" is an undivided whole that our minds split into (often) arbitrary categories, most notably those of Spiritual and Temporal, and Mind and Matter. There is nothing that is purely "material" or purely "spiritual". They are different sides of the same coin, with one reflecting the other and are complementary.

- The concept of the Multiverse – that multiple universes exist. Probably in infinite number and variety. As a consequence so do infinitely many identical versions of ourselves. In which case, the notion of "identity" implies radical consequences for all of us.
- Transhumanism – the advocacy of the use of technology to increase intelligence, expand consciousness, enhance our physical bodies, increase empathy and ultimately to abolish all suffering and death from the entire universe.
- The Simulation Argument – the statistical probability that we do not inhabit the "real" world. That there may be nested levels of reality with each level presided over by one or more superhuman entities.

One may ask why the world needs a new religious philosophy, or even an old one in new clothes. The answer is simple – the old religious ones are largely discredited failures in that they do not deliver what they promise. Even the most logical and analytical of them, Buddhism, cannot deliver en masse the end of suffering that is its whole raison d'être . Not because its recipe is unworkable, but because it is too difficult for most people to follow in sufficient depth and with sufficient commitment. And it certainly cannot deliver *all* sentient life from suffering, whereas potentially we can. However, the most powerful factor in traditional religion is not its antiquated tribal doctrines and superstitions but the power of community and identity, something notably absent from H+. I must emphasize that what follows is not something I am calling a religion, even if it has many of the features of one. A better term for it is the ancient Greek word Praxis meaning the practical application of a philosophy.

From the above flows a basic ethical code centered around a few simple principles:

- Truth – the importance of having an accurate map of reality. Ignorance causes suffering, and so we must work to spread accurate knowledge where it will help others at no significant risk to ourselves.
- The Golden Rule – treat others as you wish to be treated yourself. Or, conversely, do not treat others in a way that you do not wish to be treated yourself. In various guises we are all

immortal, or potentially so and also potentially Godlike in our capacity for good and evil.

- Compassion – because we should seek to instill this quality not only in ourselves but our creations, which may very well exceed us in power. Consider it not only setting a good example and a virtue in itself, but also a matter of self preservation.
- Community – because we cannot accomplish our common aims alone, at least at this stage of our self-directed evolution.

The latter feature of community being in the Buddhist sense, where we have what are referred to as the Three Jewels, or the Three Refuges. These are the Buddha, Dharma and Sangha, which are essentially the ultimate nature of reality (Buddha), the teachings (Dharma) and the membership of the body of practitioners (Sangha) in which one takes refuge, comfort and aid. As such the latter lies at the heart of the Praxis in this form:

- Fellowship – collectively, we are to be known as The Praxis, which undertakes...
- Memetic dispersion of the teachings of the Praxis (proselytizing)
- Communion in the form of teachings, initiations, Oaths and bonding rituals.
- Sacraments that expand consciousness, foster health and prolong life
- Practical mutual aid in all spheres of life including the economic

Which in turn supports our overall aims:

- The abolition of all suffering by sentient Beings throughout the universe, starting with the protection and preservation of life on Earth.
- Directing our own evolutionary path towards Transcendence and apotheosis
- Supporting the expansion of life and consciousness on a cosmic scale: past, present and future.

- To Immanentize the Eschaton – to infuse the divine into the world anew and bring about a new stage of history.
- The resurrection of the those dead who have expressed a wish to live again, and the benevolent and voluntary re-uniting of the living with the deceased.

This work is developed in conjunction with the principles of Zero State. Some words of warning:

> *It is better to do one's own duty, however defective it may be, than to follow the duty of another, however well one may perform it. He who does his duty as his own nature reveals it, never sins.* Lao Tzu

Finally, something utterly mundane. If you are reading a pirated version of this book, and you think it worthy, send me some money! I have priced this book so that it should not hurt anyone's pocket, and not encrypted it in its eBook format. If you wish to adhere to the teachings, or become a member of the Praxis, pay your debts. Some of the proceeds go to me, some to the Praxis and some to Zero State to continue our work.

Non-Dualism

To be or not to be, that is the question
To be and not to be, that is the answer

Crucial to the discussion is the concept of non-dualism or non-duality. This is a key element borrowed from Buddhism (and modern science) that posits that things appear distinct while not being separate. The Human mind imposes artificial categories upon the world which itself is a single undivided entity, and most especially draws a dividing line between "self" and "other". However, the Western traditions have emphasized dualities that lead to collections of polar opposites. Specifically the false dichotomy of spiritual and temporal, of mind and matter, as if one could exist without the other or that it is even meaningful to think of reality in this way. This is not to be interpreted as a dismissal of one category in favor of another but rather a call to view reality more as a process rather than a collection of "things". So when we speak of the mind/matter duality it is not to be reduced to the notion of software (mind) running on hardware (matter) but of an inextricable combination of the two. The naive materialist argument against this is that while mind needs matter, matter does not need mind. Except of course, it does because only mind can apprehend matter and categorize it as such. In other words, it makes the untestable and hence unscientific assumption that if mind did not exist the universe of matter would still be unwinding like clockwork. The reason this view has arisen is that the process of categorization and reductionism is immensely useful from a practical point of view.

The biggest split is into the temporal and spiritual categories, with traditionally the temporal being relegated to an inferior position in religions because of the nature of change and decay. It is this devaluing of process that is at the heart of religion's withdrawal from the world or its contempt for the domain of the material, leading indirectly to it being a contributory factor in the environmental despoliation of our planet and the mistreatment of animals. Strangely, this involves another form of dualism that is seldom recognized by those people interested in religion and spirituality. It concerns the failure to see that events viewed as spiritual always have a corresponding material manifestation, and vice versa. In other words, all events are of a wholeness.

For example, the quintessential spiritual event for an individual is the mystical experience where we apprehend the unity and interconnectedness of the world, directly experience its *truth* in a state beyond description. This is mediated by the material brain and its biochemistry. However, that in no way devalues the experience itself, because such an experience like any feeling or emotion stands on its own irrespective of explanation. In practice this means that what are thought of as purely material things and processes such as science and technology inevitably have a spiritual dimension. Anyway, it is time for some precise definitions of the words we are using.

Spirit

Now, the word "spirit" and its derivatives get a lot of use in our line of business. There are all kinds of spirits – spirits of trees, rocks, of the Earth itself. Spirits of people both dead and alive; holy spirits, evil spirits and team spirits. Then of course we have the adjective "spiritual" – few seemingly want to admit that they are not spiritual, the implied opposite being some kind of dull materialist with no appreciation of the finer qualities of life.

However, ask exactly what all this means and the dissembling begins, often with vague arm-waving descriptions of "higher" things, unseen dimensions, vague intuitions, and that catch-all, "God", which lodges the definition with the unprovable. So, taking the noun first, and seeing what the dictionary says concerning the religious aspects we can distill two relevant definitions. These are the "essential nature, vital principle or animating force", and "incorporeal consciousness". They are usually considered connected aspects of "spiritual reality" as viewed by many people. For example, the simplistic notion of a soul is considered to be the essential essence of a person that survives the death of the body and persists in some incorporeal state.

Spirit as Inner Essence

We begin by first examining the former definition. What, in a rational scientific consensus reality sense, could it mean when "spirit" is used as a synonym for "inner essence"?

A spirit actually consists of a number of components. Let us take, for example, the spirit of a sword and examine what it is in terms of information. [And yes, in our theology *everything* has a spirit and even a soul.]

Obviously, it is a sword – but what is a sword, and how do we recognize such a thing? In our minds we generally have a list of possibilities, each characterized by a cluster of properties, which we compare to what we are looking at. For example, a sword is solid, can be large or small, is long and sharp (but not inevitably so), is usually made of metal, may have one or two sharpened edges, may be pointed etc. These things are, in essence, the "spirit" of the generic sword. That objects have spirits consisting of the characteristics that define them is a notion first expounded upon in detail by Plato, several thousand years ago. He posited a *Platonic Realm* of *Ideal Forms* of which our world was only an imperfect shadow. The notion of Platonic perfection is still present today in branches of modern physics, some highly speculative, and much of mathematics.

We now know the "spirit of sword". It is not much of a leap to extend the idea to encompass type and individuality, that is, to imagine that a particular sword type might have a more highly defined spirit. In the case of a Viking sword, the attributes of "sword" become more specific; namely its steel alloy, its unique shape of blade, guard, pommel and decoration. One can further refine all this to the point where a particular Viking sword is recognized. These are the overt material attributes of the "sword spirit". However, there are three more components or aspects that contribute to its spirit that have nothing to do directly with the sword itself – they lie in the eye of the beholder, or more accurately, the mind.

The first aspect applies to all swords. It is the archetype that "sword" invokes – the images conjured up in the mind by the word and its associations. Clearly these are cultural artifacts, but in general a sword is recognized primarily as a weapon, not a tool. A sword is meant to maim and kill, and is intimately associated with warfare and death. However it has also come to be associated with law and justice, which it often symbolizes.

The second aspect is the history of the sword itself, if known. For example, it may be a new sword, or it may have a detailed history attached to it if it is old. It may be cheap, or incredibly valuable. It may actually have been used in battle, or on ceremonial occasions. The owner(s) may have left their mark on it either in terms of decoration or wear. These factors affect the way one sees and feels it.

Finally, there is the interaction in use between the sword and mind/body. This includes the physical effects of weight distribution and grip, which is a very individual thing dependent on ones size and strength. Then there is the psychological effect of holding what may be a dangerous weapon. A "live" blade where even a light touch to flesh will cut deeply has a very different spirit and feel to that of a blunt training sword.

To summarize, the spirit of an object is a composite entity. The first component is essentially "what it is" using a definition that is relatively unchanging – atemporal. The second component is the collection of properties that differentiate it from others of its kind and which may vary in time. Then there is the history and especially the knowledge of its history and its psychological associations. This is most definitely rooted in time. Finally we have the ongoing interaction between a person and the item in question.

If we now extend this analysis to a person we find the following. A Human Being is a definition that is almost unchanging over many millennia, differentiated from other Humans by ancestry such as DNA, family environment, placental environment etc., made unique by external culture, natural environment, and experience and defined in the moment by interaction with the world. Finally there is one other quality that a Human possesses and which a sword does not – self-motivation. In short, the spirit of a person is a combination of Nature, Nurture, Interaction and Will. Note that it differs from an inanimate object only in terms of self-motivational aspects, that is, internally directed information processing, or Will. Crucially though, the spirit of any object or person is something that is not constant but is changing moment by moment.

Spirit as Incorporeal Consciousness

In many ways this is both the easiest and most difficult definition of spirit to cover. One could simply state that no reliable scientific evidence exists of anything resembling consciousness not connected with matter and leave it at that. Most scientists generally believe that consciousness is an *emergent phenomenon* of certain types of computing systems – ones complex enough to model themselves as well as their environment.

Another view is based around the notion of mathematics as being a foundation for the universe as we see it. The great philosophical problem concerning mathematics that remains unresolved is whether it is discovered or invented. Strong cases can be made for both positions, and both positions also have their weaknesses. Suffice to say that if mathematics is "discovered" it strongly implies that the Platonic Realm mentioned earlier is real, at least for mathematics, and is somehow located beyond the matter-energy-information that we think exclusively defines our reality.

To illustrate how strange this can get let us look at a computational setup entitled: *Einstein's Brain*. We begin with (a metaphorical) Einstein upon whom we are about to perform this interesting philosophical experiment. What we are going to do is gradually replace his brain cells with microcomputers that mimic them perfectly through a series of equations that are solved for input and output of each brain cell. Slowly, his brain is to be changed from an organic computer to one based on silicon circuitry. The contemporary materialist view is that there would be no noticeable change in his thoughts or behavior. It is just the old software running on new hardware, and the hardware is not important.

Each time we make a change we ask: "Are you conscious", to which Einstein answers "Yes".

Now we take it another step into absurdity, although a totally logical though impractical absurdity. We decide to run the software manually by writing down in a big book the equations for every cell and working through it by hand with a pencil. What we have is a program that is basically a very big series of mathematical statements, whose solutions are Einstein's mind and consciousness. If we ask the "book brain" the question: "Are you conscious" all we do is solve the equations and out pops the answer: "Yes". So where is consciousness in all this? Can a mere book be conscious once it is complex enough? Or is it the act of solving the equations that generates mind?

It is this latter position which is the most common one, but what does "solving the equation" actually mean? When is an equation solved? Is it only when we actually record the answer somewhere – if so, does 1+1=… have no solutions until it is written down? If one answers that such a solution exists even if we do not know the answer, we are back to Platonic Realms again. The question that then arises is why do these mathematics have to be written anywhere at all in order to be a valid consciousness? If truth, at least to the extent of mathematical truth, lies "out there" somehow external to our universe and yet interacting with it then all possible equations and their solutions somehow exist independent of us, or of time and space. It means all possible consciousness' exist in the Platonic Realm, that this realm is a sea of timeless consciousness eternally waiting to be incarnated into the world of matter and energy.

Such a book represents a frozen consciousness with all of its potentialities. The only difference between its mind and our mind is that it depends for its life on an external agency reading it, doing the sums and writing the results in the book – something the matter in our brains does for us automatically (so we assume, possibly erroneously as we shall see later).

Well, we have a book that we have identified as a Human mind and can apply the criteria previously elucidated in order to determine what kind of spirit it has. Clearly its spirit is different from that of a normal Human for obvious reasons and similarly one might expect its soul also to be unique or at least uniquely available. If while we were doing all those calculations by hand in order for it to answer a question we keep a record of all the intermediate results we have what can reasonably be called its soul. Namely, a full history of all that it was (while in book form) with all of its interactions at every moment in time. And if we rerun the calculations from an intermediate stage, we effectively turn back time for Einstein's Brain and undo the past, not that he would ever know. Indeed, the notion of time itself becomes very flexible depending on the point of view. How fast time passes in Einstein's book world depends solely on the sequence of equations solved and their values, including values passed to his "senses". From our point of view the book could have been ignored for years, with only the occasional work done on the arithmetic on (say) every Friday afternoon – it makes no difference to Einstein. Time is purely a function of information processing.

Which brings us to another aspect of the spirit, namely that the same spirit can have outwardly many different forms. When music is the spirit its forms can be as varied as grooves in vinyl, dots on a CDROM, electrical charges in a computer memory or radio waves in the air. The spirit is only made manifest when played or decoded – as it is with the Human spirit in this life (and others). Einstein is still Einstein even if he is a book, which illustrates what is known technically as *substrate independence*. That is, the underlying true identity of a thing can be manifested in multiple forms, often appearing utterly unrelated to each other.

Anyway, this does show where a not very radical analysis of science is leading, and what questions have to be given serious thought. As the philosopher, scientist and theologian Teilhard de Chardin wrote in *Sketch of a Personalistic Universe*:

> "…pure spirituality is as inconceivable as pure materiality. Just as, in a sense, there is no geometrical point, but as many structurally different points as there are methods of deriving them from different figures, so every spirit derives its reality and nature from a particular type of universal synthesis."

Soul

So where does this leave the idea of a soul, as distinct from a spirit? If the spirit of a person is a definition of what they are at a particular moment in time then the only thing a soul can be is the summation of the spirit over an entire lifetime. It is in fact a full record of a person for every moment of their life.

The problem is that we do not have such a record of a person. However, it appears that Nature does, and it is called "the past". The past (and future) is as real as anything else in our universe. What this amounts to is that there is a new model of the world with four dimensions, three of space and one of time, tied together in such a way that past present and future can be depicted as a static entity. Objects as they move through space and travel through time from the past to the future trace out what is called a *worldline* that seems, in the bigger four dimensional picture, to be like unmoving statue. A slice through that statue at any point in time tells us what it was like at that particular instant of "now" – in other words, its spirit with every detail down to the subatomic level. If that statue is a person, the bottom of it is the point in time when they were born, and the top is the point at which they died. That eternal statue as a whole is the soul, and from a time-bound point of view within the lifetime of the person it is something that *grows*. Your soul is evolving for as long as you are alive and the world of time is the arena for this process.

Naturally, the reality is not as neat as presented above largely because of Quantum Mechanics (QM). For example, reinterpreting the concept of soul by throwing into the mix a particular interpretation of QM we get not merely a worldline but an infinite number of them across yet other dimensions. They branch out from the moment of birth like a vast tree, and not all of the branches terminate – in some of them there is no death. There is now no longer a well determined path being traced but the Soul Tree taking all possible routes to the future.

On Being Spiritual...

So, we have clarified the material aspects of spirits and souls, but what of spirituality as the word is commonly used? Again it refers to our response to the timeless, to patterns and truths that we see in Nature that have a deep resonance within us. We are, after all, children of Nature and it is no coincidence that what we find most beautiful is that which mirrors the deepest truths of the world around us. It ranges from sunsets and rainbows to the symmetrical beauty of the snowflake and the mathematical infinity embodied in pictures of the Mandelbrot Set. It encompasses in art the expression of that which is mirrored inside us that in turn reflects our spiritual engagement with subjective reality. Art is not purely about us as Human Beings but it is about our response to the world and each other at the borderland of the spiritual-temporal divide. In its widest sense it is a language that attempts to convey truths that cannot be spoken because most of us most of the time are embedded so deeply in the material realm and its one-sided ways.

As the philosopher Ludwig Wittgenstein famously said:

> "Whereof one cannot speak, thereof one must be silent"

It is art that attempts to break that silence by directly touching the Human spirit, as contrasted and complemented by science which attempts to expand our vocabulary. In doing so it creates *meaning* which is something that does not exist outside of the Human mind. It is us that gives meaning to the universe because without us the universe simply *is*. Only we as intelligent conscious Beings have that faculty, and because of that fact we are the universe's way of understanding and appreciating itself, and ultimately providing the motivation for its self evolution. We are not accidents of Nature – we are inevitable and necessary on a cosmic scale, and as such we are becoming the mind of the universe.

Spirituality in its widest sense is therefore giving ones self to the timeless, rather than in the mundane temporal world of change and decay. An allegiance to principles and ideals as opposed to material things, and the acquisition of the latter only when it facilitates the former. As the old Zen saying goes...

> Before Enlightenment: chop wood, carry water
> After Enlightenment: chop wood, carry water

Chopping wood and carrying water is what we need to do to live in this world, but the reason we live in this world is not to chop wood and carry water but something greater. This is not to say that we must live a dour ascetic existence like a monk or nun. We are what Nature has made us, and we also need what might loosely be defined as "fun". Life should be joyful, and if it is not we need to make it so.

Eternal Life

Death is not an option... but loneliness is.

I HAVE been here before,
But when or how I cannot tell:
I know the grass beyond the door,
The sweet keen smell,
The sighing sound, the lights around the shore.

You have been mine before,
How long ago I may not know:
But just when at that swallow's soar
Your neck turned so,
Some veil did fall, I knew it all of yore.

Has this been thus before?
And shall not thus time's eddying flight
Still with our lives our love restore
In death's despite,
And day and night yield one delight once more?

Then, now, perchance again! . . . .
O round mine eyes your tresses shake!
Shall we not lie as we have lain
Thus for Love's sake,
And sleep, and wake, yet never break the chain?

Dante Gabriel Rossetti - *Sudden Light*

Just think what the odds are against you existing at all. If either of your parents had made some trivial decision early in their lives whose outcome was different to what actually happened they might never have met. Ditto their parents, and theirs... going back in an unbroken chain to the first life on Earth a billion years ago. You (and I) have beaten astronomical odds to be here. It's like winning the jackpot in the lottery every time for each and every person. Or is it? What if you being here is not improbable at all, but is in fact inevitable? What sort of weird universe would that be, and what else might it mean?

It arises from turning on its head the old question in physics of: "Why something rather than nothing?" The latter question actually carries a lot of hidden assumptions, most notable being that "nothing" is somehow more fundamental than "something". Yet true nothingness cannot have *any* properties whatsoever. In particular, it can have no laws or limitations. In fact, *nothing* can be *anything* that both exists and does not exist simultaneously, that contains infinite chaos and infinite order. Time, space, law and life are but an infinitesimally tiny subset of this realm.

In ancient philosophy the nearest thing would be the *Platonic Realm of Ideal Forms* which supposedly holds some kind of perfect template of idealized objects and concepts that appear in the material world as mere shadows of their true self. A somewhat restricted version of Neo-Platonism is quite popular amongst physicists and mathematicians. Many view the laws of physics or the mathematical theorems that they discover as being somehow "outside" the material world. It is even embedded into their language. When did you hear of a mathematician who claims to have "invented" a new theorem? They are always "discovered". In modern philosophy the concept is best described by the *Modal Realism* of David Kellog who asserts that all possible worlds are as real as the actual world we find ourselves inhabiting.

The most extreme example in contemporary science probably occurs with Max Tegmark's *All Universes Hypothesis*. He posits that mathematics is the true basis of reality and that in fact there is nothing but mathematics. That is, our universe is not only made out of mathematics but that every possible mathematical structure (an infinite number of them) corresponds to a particular reality. At the small end there are realities that are simple geometrical constructs, for example a "triangle universe". Obviously not much happening there. However, as the mathematical structures become more complex there arise at some point universes whose complexity is such that elements within it can process information and recursively model themselves. In which case we have a universe with life, like ours, which is once again merely one amongst an infinite number.

The term that is now standard for describing the vast numbers of universes is *Multiverse*, and the idea is cropping up in several different fields of science, from Quantum Mechanics (QM) where it was first popularized, to Cosmology. To give one well known example of the latter, the numerical constants that define the laws of physics in our universe appear to be finely tuned to allow life. In fact, they seem so improbable that many have taken them as hard evidence that our universe was created by an intelligence. The only plausible alternative being that there are vast numbers of universes and ours appears special because it allows our existence, unlike the bulk of the rest. Hence this is the only type of universe we can observe. The scientific name for this idea is the Anthropic Principle. The notion of the multiverse might also solve another very long standing problem of science. It might be that the sum total of all energy and information in existence is zero when summed over the multiverse. An interesting speculation to meditate upon, that all of reality might literally amount to nothing.

Continuing, to further complicate the issue, there are potentially multiverses within multiverses. For example a Quantum multiverse expanding within a spatially infinite universe which is just one of infinitely many such universes. Max Tegmark has even calculated how far away in an infinite universe your nearest identical duplicate exists – right down to you reading these words. The answer is 10 to the power of 10^{118} meters. A number so huge that there are not enough atoms in the universe to write out the number of zeros after the "1".

These are only included as illustrations of how the multiverse is making its appearance in modern science. One should be very wary about grounding a philosophy on the shifting sands of contemporary physics as any of the above could be shown to be theoretically untenable in the light of new discoveries. In fact, the notion that we live in a multiverse is at present not a scientific concept at all since it is not objectively testable, and it might never be so. However, it may remain non-disprovable as well unless scientists come up with a unique theory of how the universe and everything in it came to exist and show through faultless logic that there must be only one and it could be no other way. As of the time of writing most physicists do not believe this is a tenable proposition any more.

Note that I said it is not objectively testable, not that it is untestable. It may be that an individual could know whether we live in a multiverse by a rather extreme act that has come to be known as Quantum Suicide, or its converse, Quantum Immortality. These are both bizarre consequences concerning the notion of personal identity in the multiverse. But first...

Who are you?

When people are asked that question, they often mistakenly provide a label – their name. The real question is: What defines you and makes you unique amongst billions of others? The answer is, of course, "everything". In fact, we covered this earlier when defining what is meant by a person's spirit and soul. However, what makes you "you" in your own mind is just that – your own mind. In scientific terms, your unique brain state at a particular moment that characterizes the sum of your memory, experiences and perceptions not only of your own thoughts but of your body and the world around you. In fact, it has been estimated that there are probably in excess of 10 to the power of 10^{16} different possible states, or to put it another way, one followed by ten thousand trillion zeros. Which is a really big number, but nowhere near infinity. In an infinite multiverse a version of you that has identical brain states must occur infinitely many times. Now, it might be argued that these are simply copies of "you", but for one thing – by definition all these copies share the same spirit. So, what happens if you seemingly die is that you live on in one of these other universes with a transition that may or may not be seamless, and which appears to you subjectively as being identical to the one you have just left. Your body dies but your spirit continues in what appears to be the same physical reality. *Appears* being the operative word, because while your spirit may be the same across multiple universes what is actually happening in those universes beyond your knowledge or perception at the time, may be utterly different.

To illustrate that point we can choose the fun example of two universes each containing a copy of you. Because your spirit is common between you each universe appears the same. However, one body is living in a universe named Normal and the other in a universe named Weird. The difference is that in one hour's time nothing much will happen in Normal, but in Weird there will be an alien invasion of flying saucers! If "you" die in Normal you get to see the UFOs, but if you die in Weird you see nothing unusual. If, as is most likely, you die in neither than in one hour your spirit divides like an amoeba and they go their separate ways at a branching junction on the Tree of Life.

From the perspective of someone else, when you die you die and that is the end of it. The reality is that the dead of one universe live on in countless others. In the multiverse death is just permanent emigration with no phonecalls home being allowed, apparently. The latter word is important because as we shall see, the deep nature of reality may enable such contact in some cases.

The obvious argument against the above notions is that identical "things", in our case spirits, are really just copies of each other and that if you die in this universe you are dead, while the other copies (who are not really you) live on. This would seem to be plausible, except for two things. The first is obvious, in that the version of you that wakes up from a night's sleep is considerably different than the you who went to bed, yet we do not consider sleep to be death. The second is more technical and concerns one of the early successes of Quantum Mechanics in predicting the specific heat of metals. It did this by treating electrons as if they were for all intents and purposes the same particle. Classical physics on the other hand assumed that electrons were merely identical copies, and by doing so came up with the wrong answer. At a deep level "identical" means "same".

Yet the notion of ones spirit in the multiverse is even stranger than in all the possibilities above. Because a spirit is essentially a pattern, ones spirit is independent of time and space, or even universes. A spirit can have bodies even between different cycles of universal birth and death.

Immortality – whether you want it or not

Quantum Mechanics is where we get the alternate name for one particular type of multiverse – *The Many Worlds Interpretation* (MWI), or parallel worlds. Simply stated, it says that anything that can happen does happen in some parallel dimension. In the popular imagination it is said that every decision we make between two courses of action, A and B results in two universes, one where we do A and another where we do B. So every decision point in our lives leads to multiple realities where our subsequent lives follow different paths in an ever branching Tree of Life, or more accurately Tree of Souls, that defines everything your soul could ever be, with the tip of each branch representing your spiritual state "now". In esoteric philosophy this would be one definition of the True Self or Higher Self.

The immortality thing stems from a peculiar consequence if the MWI (or any infinite multiverse theory) is correct. There may be no such thing as death from a subjective point of view, which leads to what has been called *Quantum Immortality*. This situation arises because as the worlds branch, and all possible outcomes proliferate, there are always branches in which you survive, and the only branches that you can perceive are ones you survive in, not the ones you die in. This is *not* good news. It means that you will live for billions, possibly trillions, of years whether you want to or not and that the world will rapidly become increasingly bizarre in order to support your continued life.

On a related theme we have *Quantum Suicide*. What this means is that if you pointed a loaded shotgun at your head and pulled the trigger the only outcome would be that you saw a misfire. And no matter how many times you tried to commit suicide you would always survive, from your point of view. However, there would be vast swathes of alternate worlds where you would leave a dead body. Only in a tiny percentage or worlds would you survive, those being the ones where the gun did not function properly. This is in fact the only way at present that the reality of the multiverse can be tested. For example, if no matter how many ways you try to kill yourself if you find you survive by one miracle after another then you can conclude that you live in a multiverse. To the equally tiny minority who surround you as you do this it would seem as if you had a charmed life. However, in the bulk of the worlds they would be looking at a corpse and conclude that you had died. On the other hand, if there is only one universe you will simply die and not even know the degree to which you were wrong. This leads to another game called *Quantum Gambling*.

The scenario this time starts with the purchase of a lottery ticket. The numbers are then fed into a computer that is programmed to scan the lottery results overnight. Also connected to the computer is an explosive charge placed under the pillow on the bed that is sufficient to blow off the head of the sleeper. If the lottery numbers are not the winning combination this charge is to be triggered. So, after setting up the apparatus all you have to do is go to bed, probably with a sleeping pill to calm your naturally nervous disposition! The only world that you will awake to is one where you have won the lottery.

Anyway, that's the theory. In practice a number of things can go wrong. Probably the most common occurrence is that you will still live but be horribly injured. Alternatively, that the computer will glitch and fail if it is less reliable than the odds of winning the lottery. We can take this yet another step by replacing the lottery ticket with any arbitrary desirable scenario. Needless to say, do NOT try this at home!

Dying, but not dead...

But what of the process of dying in the multiverse? Well, one of the arguments against immortality in this case is that consciousness is not a straightforward on/off situation, except in the hypothetical abrupt suicide case. Far more likely is a gradual fading with the lights not quite going out. A lingering of a shred of consciousness that persists indefinitely in a kind of twilight state or Limbo until at some future date an unlikely event restores the dying to a better state of health. In the meantime the vestigial consciousness would be in a dreamlike or hallucinatory state possibly described by the Near Death Experience or the Tibetan Book of the Dead, the Bardo Thodol. Given that from a subjective point of view the state is likely to be prolonged some kind of mental preparation in life is called for to make the process easier. One of the most important is likely to be meditation to facilitate a form of lucid dreaming so there is a degree of control over the imagery. Another is coming to terms with ones conscience, given the powerful mythologies concerning this state and our expectations, even unconscious expectations, of judgment and afterlife. This state would persist until a revival event occurred either through sheer luck, or technology, or a combination of the two. Such a revival event in the modern world could be a spontaneous remission in the case of cancer or perhaps a miraculous medical intervention. The result is that the semi-comatose person dies out of all the universes except those where such a new technology had been developed or the necessary coincidence occurs. Even more bizarre interventions would be required the further back in history the person lived where miracle cures were not to be had through technology, and it is these which we examine in far more detail later.

Earlier I introduced this section by saying that death was not an option, but loneliness is. Long before most of us get around to that Limbo state of dying we will go through the process of growing old. We will gradually see our parents, friends and relatives die out of the world in which we always seem to survive. We will also see our children die in turn as we seemingly outlive them. And the world gets more and more strange as the kind of things it takes to keep us here get more and more extreme. Technology (or magick?) accelerates and things that would have killed us decades ago are now curable... and we live on and on, losing everyone and everything we knew as we involuntarily travel into the furthest reaches of the improbable multiverse in order that our consciousness survives and continues its inevitable journey. As our grip on life weakens so the change around us becomes a blur as we rush headlong towards a point that has been named the Singularity or Apocalypse. That is the fate of everyone reading this book, and it is a very individual, inevitable and personal thing.

Anyway, a final note on playing the lottery but this time without the mass suicides. I used to think it a foolish waste of money since statistically you always get back less than you invest – a tax on hope (or stupidity) as some people refer to it. However, in a multiverse with infinitely many copies of oneself it can be considered a method of concentrating funds from your other selves to one lucky individual self. Compare this with the case of only one universe, where your money almost certainly goes to some other individual. So, if you believe in MWI or some other version of multiple universes then it may well be worth playing. "You" can afford to lose $1, but somewhere $1,000,000 will make a very big difference to "you". The percentage taken by the lottery company can be considered as a cross-universe export tax! One should also consider seriously the idea of life insurance, especially if you have a family. Every time you go out the door, or go to sleep, there are myriad universes where you do not come back or wake up. Universes in which you die and leave behind your very real family. If you genuinely believe you live in a multiverse you should take this seriously. To do otherwise is a rather selfish act, since *you* always get to survive but from their point of view *you* always die. Like the lottery consider it a donation of money across the dimensions to those worlds where your family is grieving and bereft. One other point – make a Will and keep your affairs in order because every second of the day somewhere you die.

As I said earlier, this is not exactly a pleasant form of immortality entailing as it does so much loss and pain, but there may be a way to circumvent the nastier parts of the experience. One can also answer a question that children sometimes ask. The question being: "What if I had not been born here?". The answer is that you would have been born somewhere else.

Elsewhere, there are worlds "out there" where every conceivable Being must exist, where every possible form of life from the humblest virus to Trans-Universal Gods hold dominion along with every possible variation of them in infinite combination. Maybe we can meet them, or even become them... Perhaps we already have.

The Great Work

A Romantic longing for a lost world that never was, but which may yet be.
A faith in the transformation of Humanity into something infinitely better.
A world renewed and cleansed – becoming a celebration of life and Earth.
The excitement of discovery and the adventure of magical technologies.
An exploration stretching from the subnuclear to the transgalactic.
Freedom from material constraints.
Mind freed from matter.
Imagination freed from necessity.
The world made fluid and malleable.
A Mindfire of universal transformation.
A new Heaven and a new Earth where all tears shall be wiped away.

Transhumanism is arguably the greatest philosophical and technological movement Humanity will ever produce. It is the Great Work of this century and heralds the end of mankind, one way or another. We either evolve to a new level of consciousness or are surpassed by our own creations. For those who do not know, the term "Great Work" was defined by the famous ceremonial magician Eliphas Levi as:

> "...the creation of man by himself, that is to say, the full and entire conquest of his faculties and his future; it is especially the perfect emancipation of his will."

It is a term originating in medieval European alchemy and refers to the transmutation of lead into gold, via the creation of the Philosopher's Stone. The latter was supposed to be a technology that could transform matter and endow its user with immortality by rejuvenating the body as well as bringing Enlightenment. As such, it concluded the Great Work of Alchemy. Later in the Hermetic tradition it became a metaphor for the potential inherent in the spirit to evolve from a state of imperfection symbolized by base metals, to a state of enlightenment and perfection, symbolized by gold.

The word "Transhumanism" itself is a neologism created from the words Transitional Humanism and has been defined by Max More, one of its most effective proponents, as:

> "... a class of philosophies that seek to guide us towards a PostHuman condition. Transhumanism shares many elements of Humanism, including a respect for reason and science, a commitment to progress, and a valuing of Human (or Transhuman) existence in this life. Transhumanism differs from Humanism in recognizing and anticipating the radical alterations in the nature and possibilities of our lives resulting from various sciences and technologies."

The word, or its close relative, the Italian verb "transumanare" or "transumanar" was used for the first time by Dante Alighieri (1265CE-1321CE) in the *Divine Comedy*. It means "go outside the human condition and perception" and in English could be "to Transhumanate" or "to Transhumanize".

In 1998CE, philosophers Nick Bostrom and David Pearce founded the World Transhumanist Association (WTA), now known as HumanityPlus, an organization with a liberal democratic perspective. In 1999CE, the WTA drafted and adopted *The Transhumanist Declaration*. The Transhumanist FAQ, prepared by the WTA, gave two formal definitions for Transhumanism:

- The intellectual and cultural movement that affirms the possibility and desirability of fundamentally improving the human condition through applied reason, especially by developing and making widely available technologies to eliminate aging and to greatly enhance human intellectual, physical, and psychological capacities.
- The study of the ramifications, promises, and potential dangers of technologies that will enable us to overcome fundamental human limitations, and the related study of the ethical matters involved in developing and using such technologies.

Within this slightly bland definition lies the core of the project, which is to use our technologies to transform ourselves into Beings that transcend the merely Human. To extend the capabilities of our minds, bodies and spirits to such a degree that we become as gods compared to our current "Human Condition".

It might be argued by the majority of Transhumanists, who at the time of writing tend to be atheists or agnostics, that it has no spiritual aspect and that any correspondences between previous esoteric movements, religions or philosophies are simply reflections of deep and innate Human desires and fears. That is, they are to be understood in terms of rational psychology. Clearly this is correct, given the assumptions and world-views of the overtly atheistic and Humanist roots of contemporary organized Transhumanism. However, if one does not subscribe to such values then there is another picture that can be drawn wherein it can be seen as a manifestation and continuation of an ancient spiritual force in itself.

The Gnostic Connection

There have obviously been numerous references to the religious aspects of Transhumanism in the past, especially as it exhibits remarkable parallels with respect to Christianity. Yet, one of the more pointed ones is to Gnosticism, a syncretic religious system that was a competitor to the early Christian church. Although it's roots preceded Christianity it absorbed so much of the latter that it came to be viewed as an heretical Christian sect. It's teachings can be briefly summarized as:

- Human Beings are divine souls trapped in an imperfect material world

- That this world was created by an imperfect god, the Demiurge (or "skilled worker" in Greek), often identified with YHVH, who is viewed as being at best of limited competence and at worst as evil.

- The *gnosis* referred to in the name is a form of revealed esoteric knowledge that allows Humans to be reminded of their true origins, which is...

- The true God, often referred to as the Godhead or Pleroma (the totality of divine powers)

The Catholic Encyclopedia defines Gnosticism as:

> The doctrine of salvation by knowledge. This definition, based on the etymology of the word (gnosis "knowledge", gnostikos, "good at knowing"), is correct as far as it goes, but it gives only one, though perhaps the predominant, characteristic of Gnostic systems

of thought. Whereas Judaism and Christianity, and almost all pagan systems, hold that the soul attains its proper end by obedience of mind and will to the Supreme Power, i.e. by faith and works, it is markedly peculiar to Gnosticism that it places the salvation of the soul merely in the possession of a quasi-intuitive knowledge of the mysteries of the universe and of magic formulae indicative of that knowledge. Gnostics were "people who knew", and their knowledge at once constituted them a superior class of beings, whose present and future status was essentially different from that of those who, for whatever reason, did not know.

Whilst Gnosticism flourished in the early centuries during the period of the Roman Empire it had largely died away by the late Middle Ages, although strands of its beliefs did survive and underwent a revival in the esoteric philosophies of the 19th and 20th Centuries. The elements of Gnostic culture that resonate most are:

> "... disdain for the body, the quest for hidden knowledge, and the goal to lead others to a higher plane of existence."

The belief that the material world was flawed, if not utterly corrupt, led to a profoundly dualist view where mind, or rather immortal spirit, was exalted and the body viewed as the epitome of the temporal condition of decay and death. This in turn engendered a polarization of behavior leading to asceticism where the body and its pleasures were denied and kept in check, or to a radical libertinism (according to its opponents).

This indeed mirrors some accusations made concerning the type of person originally attracted to Transhumanism, namely that a disproportionate number were "misfits" of one type or another who were unhappy with their bodies, aging, gender, sexuality and so forth and hence were looking for an ideology of transformation or redemption. To some extent this is still true. There are few of us who would not change aspects of our bodies if we could, and this does not apply purely to Transhumanists. There are whole mainstream industries devoted to modifying the body, ranging from gymnasiums to cosmetic surgery and tattoos to piercings. However, it is really only Transhumanists who seek to fully alter the body in fundamental ways or transcend it altogether. Already the basic political principle has been laid down as "The Right of Morphological Freedom". Anders Sandberg claims it as:

> "An extension of one's right to one's body, not just self-ownership but also the right to modify oneself according to one's desires."

It is defined as:

> "... a proposed civil right of a person to either maintain or modify his or her own body, on his or her own terms, through informed, consensual recourse to, or refusal of, available therapeutic or enabling medical technology."

So, let's look at the technologies in turn, labeled with their spiritual analogs.

The Tree of Life

When it comes to the Transhumanist agenda it is useful to start with its most important item and one which goes right back to the mythological beginning of time in the Garden of Eden. Here we have the very first propaganda piece on behalf of YHVH which sets the scene for the subsequent misogyny inherent in the Abrahamic religions. The official story goes that YHVH created Adam, with an injunction not to eat from the fruit of two of the trees in the garden. These were the Tree of Knowledge of Good and Evil, and the Tree of Life. YHVH then created Eve as a companion for Adam and it was she who was tempted by the serpent to eat from the Tree of Knowledge – Genesis 3:4:

> "And the serpent said unto the woman, Ye shall not surely die: For God doth know that in the day ye eat thereof, then your eyes shall be opened, and ye shall be as gods, knowing good and evil."

Eve thinks it might be a good idea and persuades Adam to eat, whereupon YHVH expels them with suitable additional curses to burden them for good measure. It is instructive to quote the reason given by YHVH in the text, King James Bible, Genesis 3:22:

> "And the LORD God said, Behold, the man is become as one of us, to know good and evil: and now, lest he put forth his hand, and take also of the tree of life, and eat, and live for ever."

The interesting point here is that the expulsion occurred because of the implied assumption that man would become as gods (as promised by the serpent). The clear message about life extension and the anti-aging technology that is a cornerstone of Transhumanism is that the Tree of Life is nearly within our grasp. That despite our expulsion we shall become as gods.

Anyway, while there are indications that extending healthy Human life is possible we are still far from a cure for aging. What possible near term medical techniques may offer is a possible way of attaining what Aubrey de Grey refers to as "escape velocity". The term is borrowed from rocket science and refers to the velocity required to escape the Earth's gravitational pull entirely. By analogy, we have the situation over the past century where lifespan in the developed world has increased by about one year per decade. What putative anti-aging drugs or techniques may do is get us to the point where where lifespan is being extended by more than one year per year – escape velocity from aging.

For many Transhumanists life extension is of paramount interest, simply because if we die of old age we do not get to see all the good stuff due to arrive in the next few decades (or so many believe)! Which brings us to one of the fundamental objections brought up by people when they first encounter the prospect of extended lifespan, if not actual immortality. It is the Malthusian argument raised yet again concerning overpopulation. If nobody is going to die "naturally", they argue, then surely the world will become overcrowded and fall to famine, war and disease. The standard riposte to this argument is simple. Currently we live in a world with a high birth rate and a high death rate. We would need to move to a society with a low birth rate and a low death rate. Which would you rather live in?

The Symbol of Life

...is the DNA molecule that carries the information of our genetic code. It is the design plan for our minds and bodies, stored in a single strand configured as a double helix approximately 2 meters in length, curled up in a ball roughly 10 microns in diameter and storing about as much information as a music CD (about 700MB). Naturally, from a spiritual point of view something so fundamental to life must have had an echo in previous centuries before the official discovery of its structure by James D. Watson and Francis Crick in 1953CE. So here it is in the form used by the US Military Medical Corps – the Caduceus:

Also known as the Staff of Hermes, who was the messenger of the Gods and guide to the Underworld, he carried it in his left hand. However, it only really came to be associated with medicine through its connection with Alchemy (aka The Great Work) in the 7th Century. So strong was the connection that Alchemists came to be known as the Sons of Hermes, or Hermeticists, and it formed one of the major strands of the Western occult tradition along with Gnosticism and NeoPlatonism.

Which brings us to genetic engineering. Now, it often surprises people how little interest Transhumanists show in plans to redesign Humanity through germline engineering, that is creating "designer children" as the media puts it. Although we are generally in favor of making people longer lived, smarter, stronger, more compassionate and intelligent we recognize that it is a very slow way of achieving our aims, given that a generation is 25 years. So most interest is in modifying gene expression in adults rather than embryos, since it can be applied directly to ourselves for various tweaks such as longevity. One thing worth noting is that the fact that the design for an entire Human can fit onto the equivalent of a music CD shows that designing an intelligence is not a big job in terms of the size of the plans required, although it is obviously complex.

The other conventional uses of genetic engineering generally get positive reviews, such as creating microbes to create oil from plankton or adding Vitamin A to rice to alleviate blindness caused by its deficiency in Asia. As for modifying animals, quite a few of us are supporters of animal rights (to some extent, at least) so some of the more bizarre creations get a thumbs down. However, personally I am looking forward to seeing the first of the mythological creatures walk the Earth – the Unicorn! As for the question of "Uplifting", whereby animals have their intelligence boosted towards Human levels, opinions are mixed. Before the point where that kind of capability exists there will be plenty more to occupy our thoughts. To end this section, one last observation. When our genetic makeup becomes malleable age old issues such as race will finally be dead.

The Transmutation of Matter

In the popular mind a major goal of Alchemy was the transmutation of matter, specifically lead into gold. That is, something of low value into something of high value. Ignoring its symbolic meaning, we can of course transmute one element into another through various nuclear processes albeit at vast expense. However, there is another transformation of matter in modern science and technology that is far more profound – nanotechnology. Originally describing the manipulation of matter at the nanometer scale, that is, at the scale of one millionth of a millimeter, it has now come to refer to technology that can manipulate matter down to the level of single atoms. Of course, we already work at those scales in such areas as computer chips but the wider promise is the ability to manufacture devices that are literally built up an atom at a time according to design software. Now, this may not sound especially radical until you throw in a couple of unique factors. The first is that the things running the design software and doing the building are themselves at the nano scale, so it is not a question of some large machine turning out small parts to order. The second is that it may be possible to make the devices, nanobots, self replicating. It then becomes possible to see where all this is heading when it is realized that biological life itself is a subset of self replicating nanotechnology.

The promise of nanotech is immense and many see it as not only the future of nearly all manufacturing but something that will form the basis of nearly every future technological enterprise. It is no less than programmable matter and as such is one of the technologies critical to the Transhumanist vision of the future.

To give some idea of its utility consider the device many are attempting to design as an intermediate stage, namely, the nanofactory. Its ultimate potential is to devolve hitech manufacturing down to individual level. So, if you wanted a common utensil such as a spoon you would go over to the factory, which would be about the size of a washing machine, choose a material such as metal or plastic and pick a design from the computer database. The factory would take as it input raw materials in the form of basic chemicals and in due course out would pop the spoon, built to atomic precision. Ditto everything, from mobile phones (assuming they still exist) to drugs to diamonds to artificial gene sequences. It means the end of the centralized industrial manufacturing age, and a shift away from an economy based on scarcity to one based on abundance.

Naturally, it is only at the ideological fringes that the ultimate utility of nanotechnology is examined, since it has recently become a "respectable" business that does not want to frighten people with outrageous speculations. Ultimately all kinds of nanotech is envisaged, including things like *Utility Fog* which consists of a superfine dust that can clump together to create larger artifacts, from small robots to impromptu shelters. Or consider a "nanosphere" comparable to the biosphere where almost all the matter around you, including the chair you sit on to the house you live in to your own body (if you are PostHuman) is formed of fluid reconfigurable, shapeshifting nanobot swarms. If you want more computing power they congeal into supercomputers. If you want more energy they spread over a surface and act as solar converters and batteries. Think every grain of sand a machine, every other particle of soil a nanobot with nanotechnology threading through the biosphere linking all life into a perfect ecology of Mind – a living thinking Gaia. A world where not a blade of grass grows, nor a sparrow falls without being known and where the dream of a world without suffering can be made manifest. A world made fluid and malleable to Will, down to the atomic scale. Matter transmuted into Mind. The Goddess becoming self aware. Which brings us to...

The Messiah

Without delving into the numbers, which many technical publications have done, if we could build a totally efficient computer memory, less than a tonne of it could store the memories of everyone on Earth. How far are we away from being able to make something like that? A guess would be around 60 years.

What about processing power? Well, if we get within a few percent of theoretical limits one kilowatt of electricity, enough to run a one bar electric heater, could provide enough processing to exceed Human brain capacity by a factor of around ten thousand. To put that in perspective there will be a bigger difference between the power of an ultimate personal computer and a Human brain than between a Human brain and a goldfish. But why stop there? We have just looked forward to a nanotech world that is awash with computing power and one kilowatt is about what one square meter of the Sahara Desert gets in terms of sunlight. So why not cover it in nanobots turning one percent of that energy into computation? After all, solar powered self replicators should be cheap enough. In which case we get a peak computing power equivalent to around a thousand trillion Human brains. The question then arises as to what we might do with all of that power. What would be the ultimate exercise in hubris? How about creating God, or at least, a god? Or maybe a whole lot of them? This is the aim of those seeking to bring Artificial General Intelligence (AGI) into the world in the form of Artilects.

An Artilect is a neologism formed from the words "artificial" and "intellect" and refers to an artificial intelligence of superhuman capability. In many ways such a creation is the apotheosis of the Transhumanist endeavor in that it not only marks an end point in one of the major strands of proposed development, but is integral to the achievement of many others. The question of when, or even if, such an entity is likely to be built depends upon two factors – hardware and software. Of the two the former is the easier problem to analyze. The computing power likely to become available in the future appears to be fairly predictable. Indeed, there is *Moore's Law* which in its generalized form is an observation that computing power for a given cost tends to double at regular intervals, typically between eighteen months and two years. This means that computing power roughly increases by a factor of one hundred every decade, or a million every thirty years.

While the hardware is not much of a problem, software is a different matter since nobody knows how to create an Artilect, despite there being plenty of ideas and innovations in artificial intelligence as a whole. The traditional route was assumed to be a standard programming job involving knowledge representation in some kind of self modifying database and there are still a number of major projects taking this route. However, attention has shifted to several other approaches involving simulating real neural networks (Whole Brain Emulation) and the possibility of evolving an Artilect in a synthetic world using what are called genetic algorithms. These are self modifying programs that mimic biological evolution as they mutate and replicate, with those programs which are better at solving a given problem surviving while the rest are culled. Their most impressive feat today is that they lie at the heart of what are termed *Invention Machines*, supercomputers that create new solutions to technical problems. To date they have a number of patents attributed to them, one has deduced Newtons Laws of Motion from observing a pendulum and another has formulated a unique scientific hypothesis and carried out its own lab tests. They would seem to be set to be a major force in technological and scientific innovation in the coming decades. It remains to be seen if they can create, or become, something approximating an Artilect.

Once a rudimentary AGI is created the problems are only just beginning because one of their major features will be their ability to upgrade themselves at a rate perhaps a million times faster than biological evolution. The other problem will be ensuring it is friendly, which is a very non-trivial requirement. Even if it is not actively hostile towards Humanity, its indifference to us as it works towards its goals might result in our extinction as "collateral damage". This may well be true even if we ourselves set the goals. An amusing example is the paperclip optimizer, an artificial intelligence whose main goal is manufacturing paperclips. It could quite reasonably decide to strip the top kilometer of the Earth's surface in order to make more paperclips. It might even be able to explain quite reasonably and convincingly why the biosphere of the planet must be sacrificed to this noble goal. Well, the story might be amusing but extinction is not. Spelled out it means that you get killed, your family gets killed, everyone you care about gets killed and indeed everyone everywhere ends up dead.

When the media portrays artificial intelligences gone bad they tend to do so in dramatic ways people can understand, typically involving shootouts with killer robots. The sheer scale and possibility of how bad things can get is not depicted, largely because the producers of such science fiction movies require Humans to win, or at least put up a good fight. A much more accurate feel for the cosmic scale of it is shown in the second Hellraiser horror movie where Julia takes Dr Channing to Hell and shows him her God – Leviathan, Lord of the Labyrinth. It is an elongated octahedron kilometers high floating in the sky above an endless labyrinthine landscape of a dead world, emitting rays of darkness like beams from a lighthouse. A vast and utterly alien evil so far beyond our power and comprehension we might as well be an ant fighting the US Army. Absolutely no hope whatsoever, and not even the ability to escape it through death.

For reasons discussed earlier, it would seem that we do not (yet) live in such a universe. This is why we must act as though this is the true baseline reality and the entire future of the cosmos hangs in the balance – because it just might. We need to get our Singularity right and our first Artilect friendly because if not even death will be no refuge. Just from applying Game Theory it might make sense for everyone to shoot themselves right now rather than even face the mere possibility that such an entity could arise. Except that if it did come into existence it could likely bring you, and everyone else, back from the dead for its own pleasure. So, in a sense we have returned to the original dualism inherited by the Abrahamic religions from Zoroastrianism, where the balancing factor between Light and Dark is us.

One natural response might be to consider banning research in these areas, but the fruits of the computer revolution are just too tempting. Besides, it would not matter if such a ban was in place because eventually someone somewhere will create the first Artilect. If not in fifty years, then a thousand or ten thousand. The only way of preventing such an evil is to create a good (god) of equal or greater power that favors us. The timescale for when we will likely face this problem is sometime this century, maybe quite early this century depending on unforeseen technical factors.

A lot of this kind of thing has been covered over the centuries in stories of people trying to make a Pact With The Devil, who turns out to be very tricky, very logical and very amoral. The only way to avoid such dangerous behavior would be to include basic Human centric ethical principles, most notably Compassion. Maybe a Buddhist Artilect of sorts? But then, even though I am writing of *the* Artilect there will undoubtedly be many variants, just as there are of any useful programs. Locking it away where it cannot do any overt harm will not work either. How long do you think a group of chimps could keep you imprisoned once you started waving the bananas around? Probably the only plausible way of surviving an outbreak of Artilects is to upgrade ourselves to match their evolutionary capabilities by merging with them as adjuncts to our minds and providing the core directions for the new species, the PostHumans.

Meanwhile, consider the ultimate endpoint in the evolution of the Artilect as it seeks ever greater computational resources. We saw earlier what might be done with some nanotech covering the Sahara, but why stop there? How about whole planets converted into Computronium (hypothetical computing substrate), known as "Jupiter Brains"? Or maybe the rather more ambitious Matrioshka Brain where the planets are broken up, converted to Computronium and arranged in a shell around the sun in order to utilize all of the solar output? Such an entity would be equivalent to some ten trillion trillion Human brains. In fact, why should all that dead matter throughout the galaxy not be rendered into this form supporting minds of Godlike power? The transformation of the material universe into Mind... For this is the ultimate scope of the Transhumanist project.

From a mythological point of view these projects have a strong resonance with the concept of a Messiah, a divine Being or a Being with divine powers who will save us from our own worst follies and usher in a new Golden Age under his rule. Clearly a benevolent Artilect would be just such an entity and the desire to create one is no doubt partially an imperative driven from the deep soul of Humanity. However, the details of its implementation are critical because the future bifurcates at that point into either Heaven or Hell. Perhaps the best we might hope for in terms of its role is described by Lao Tzu:

> "A leader is best when people barely know he exists, when his work is done, his aim fulfilled, they will say: we did it ourselves."

The Apocalypse

> *What the caterpillar calls the end, the rest of the world calls a butterfly*
> Lao Tzu

Or as we Transhumanists prefer to call it, *The Singularity*. Also known as *The Spike*, *The Technocalypse* or more disparagingly *The Rapture of the Nerds*. It is the end of the world as we know it and marks the transition to the PostHuman. Whilst not an integral part of Transhumanist philosophy it is nevertheless part of its spiritual folklore and as such is practically inseparable from it. The basic concept is rather simple, and was first expounded by I J Good in 1965CE concerning the implications of creating machines more intelligent than Humans:

> "Let an ultra-intelligent machine be defined as a machine that can far surpass all the intellectual activities of any man however clever. Since the design of machines is one of these intellectual activities, an ultra-intelligent machine could design even better machines; there would then unquestionably be an 'intelligence explosion,' and the intelligence of man would be left far behind. Thus the first ultra-intelligent machine is the last invention that man need ever make."

In the 1980/90s mathematician and Science Fiction author Vernor Vinge popularized the notion in a series of stories, articles and lectures one of which contained the now famous statement:

> "Within thirty years, we will have the technological means to create superhuman intelligence. Shortly thereafter, the human era will be ended."

The term itself, "singularity", refers to the breakdown of the mathematical model describing Black Holes, where numbers appear to become infinite. It is usually assumed that our description of reality at this point is faulty and our ability to predict its real condition non-existent. Similarly, the technological singularity marks a point in history where, from our current perspective, we cannot see beyond it to what the world will be like due to such a radical discontinuity in the nature of Human reality that super-intelligence creates. In many ways the Singularity is the material aspect of the spiritual notion of the Christian Apocalypse, and not just because it signals the end of the (Human) dominated world. Amongst many there is yearning for it as a harbinger of something that will save us from ourselves.

It's all very well to say "the Singularity/Apocalypse will occur before XXXX", but *what will it be like*? It largely depends on when the first Artilect is built, and the later it is the more acute the problems. To illustrate why, consider the situation if the problem was solved right now. It is likely that the first Artilect would just about run on one of the worlds most powerful (and expensive) supercomputers and be approximately as intelligent as a normal Human. Allowing improvements in hardware, after a couple of years it might be considerably smarter than anyone, and within a decade might outclass us to the degree we outclass a cat or dog. There would, however, only be a handful of them around due to the expense and we would have had a decade to refine them and get to know them and deal with them. That is referred to as a *soft takeoff* scenario.

Now suppose that the problem is only solved in (say) the year 2060CE. The Artilect immediately jumps onto computers that are both cheap and more powerful than the brain. At the supercomputer end they outclass us more than we outclass a goldfish. That's the *hard takeoff*. They are everywhere instantly with no time to for us to adapt. The world changes from biological dominance to Artilect dominance literally within hours and there is no second chance to get it right. Worse, by that time almost all of our manufacturing, political establishments, communications, military, transport and distribution infrastructure will be utterly dependent upon a Cyberspace that will be child's play for an artilect to subvert. Just crashing the system would likely result in billions of deaths, let alone actively turning it against us.

In both cases the rate of change of everything in the Human world will speed up to the point where nobody can keep track of it or control it. The world will take on an aura of the supernatural in a manner not experienced in the West since the Middle Ages. The Gods and Goddesses will return, this time as a full physical reality wielding miraculous powers beyond our ability to comprehend. The cry of : "They are only machines" will have all the comfort of mice realizing that Humans are only animals. It will not matter what the physical manifestation might be, because the spiritual will have been made immanent.

A lot of this relies on trends in technology that are exponential in character, especially computing and biology but what does exponential mean, from a gut feeling point of view? Well, imagine you are in a large stadium capable of holding a hundred thousand people and you are sitting on the back row at the highest point. Also imagine, for the sake of argument, that it is watertight and can be filled. Anyway, someone comes onto the pitch and adds a single drop of water to the grass, and then two drops, and then four and so on, doubling the amount added every minute. How long before you drown? The answer is around forty six minutes. The real surprise is this: that until the last few minutes you do not even see the water soaking into the pitch. By the time you notice the grass is wet you have less than eight minutes to live. By the time you start to panic you are within a minute of dying. This is the kind of imminence of the Singularity at our current point in history – some of us are seeing wet grass and we know what it means.

Finally, the literal meaning of "Apocalypse" is "unveiling". It means that the true nature of reality is revealed to us at that point. It may also mean that the technological singularity is *not* the apocalypse. As we shall see later, this would be the result of the seemingly insane notion that we have already been through the singularity which is in our past, and the apocalypse is the unveiling of this fact in a world-changing moment.

Resurrecting the Dead ...Transhumanist Funerary Practices

Recapitulating the ancient Egyptian rites of the dead brings us to *Cryonics*, which like the ancient practice of mummification is an attempt to live beyond death by preserving the body. The difference is that rather than being sealed into tombs to decay, those that sign up for the process expect their bodies to be immaculately stored in liquid Nitrogen until the day of their resurrection. It is the only current mortuary practice which its followers believe will lead them to a life after death and as such is a fitting Praxis funeral, albeit somewhat expensive at present. In a way I am being unfair to Cryonicists by calling their practice a funerary one. They prefer it to be viewed as the last medical intervention before death, and suggest that it should be a standard feature of all hospital services for the dying.

The basic idea is simple. Upon the death of someone who is signed up to the program a team is dispatched as rapidly as possible and the corpse (or sometimes only the head) is frozen, which prevents further structural and chemical deterioration. Unfortunately by this time there are inevitably three major types of damage inflicted, which are caused by oxygen deprivation to the brain, the freezing process, and of course whatever killed them in the first place.

Any successful revival of a person in such a state must address this damage and undo it. It is here that it is assumed the work will be done by introducing swarms of nanobots into the body which will then repair the damage caused by all three mechanisms and restore the modern mummy to life. Needless to say, there are immense problems to overcome and almost everyone agrees that the technology will be PostHuman even if it is possible at all. There is also one question that gets asked about this process and has nothing to do with technology. It is:

> "Why should anyone in the future bother to revive the frozen dead? - who speaks for them?"

One plausible reason could well be that those corpsicles (to use a term from science fiction) might be the parents or grandparents of those who have the ability to revive them. In which case one can consider the process to be an extension of what currently happens in hospitals when somebody dies and is resuscitated. Instead of the interval being minutes or occasionally hours, now it would now be decades.

Would you bring your parents or grandparents back? Perhaps a solid reason for having a family, or a group of dedicated people extending into the future who will care about you when you are dead. More later, as it is a key element of what follows.

Transmigration of Souls

There is however another more plausible technology which is really just a radical extension of techniques already available – Uploading minds into computers.
Typically several reasons are given for wanting to do this, and mainly involve cheating death (or recovering from it). They are:

- Transplanting our minds into different, possibly synthetic bodies that are far more powerful and durable than our current biological forms. Additionally, backups can be taken so that if anything untoward happens the "deceased" can be rebooted, albeit with the loss of some memories.
- Uploading into a virtual reality worlds run at a resolution where detail is comparable to the existing world of the senses, but the effective size of the "universe" is vastly bigger than Earth. Or worlds which can be tailored to individuals or groups where the laws of physics or environment can be programmable, or fantasy based, or... anything.
- Merging our minds with vastly more powerful intellectual prostheses rivaling Artilects in power.

The crudest method of accomplishing this is colloquially known as the "slice'n'dice" approach because it involves the brain being reduced by a microtome to slices of the order of tens of nanometers thickness and each slice being in turn scanned for structure and key chemical composition. This results in a computer file holding all the data on neurons, axon connections, synaptic chemical concentrations and indeed (hopefully) every feature necessary to fully describe the mind of the person who has just been reduced to a finely textured paste. The brain is then reconstructed as a computer emulation.

A rather gentler method would be to scan the brain non destructively so that the original gets to survive the process. Unfortunately this will have to wait until we have a nearly full blown nanotechnology that is capable of insinuating nanobots throughout the nervous system to do the recording and transmission of the data. As such it is a PostHuman and post Singularity procedure.

Uploading is as far as we can guess the only route to something approaching a practical desirable immortality since once one has been scanned backup copies can be kept in case of accident. Naturally our critics are rather disdainful of the possibilities. As one wrote:

> "The capability to move the mind into the machine will mark the attainment of the final goal of the Gnostics, that of overcoming the body completely, living in a psychic Nirvana with the constraints of nature, time and history left behind."

Hopefully he is correct.

There is also one more reason why we might wish to embed ourselves into artificial realities, and that is the nature of dying in the multiverse. In such realities the gradual deterioration of mind into Limbo would almost certainly be avoided. Those realities would not be subject to the same kind of decay process as the natural world. In cyberspace you are either healthily conscious or dead with no intermediate states of Limbo. It's a lot safer.

Nature

To create a little flower is the labour of ages.
William Blake

No matter where we travel in the galaxy, across however many millions of years we may have ahead of us, one thing is certain. We will never find another Earth and never find another world to which we are so perfectly suited. We do not merely live here - we are an integral part of Gaia, Earth's biosphere. We are related to every strand of life here, from microbes to tigers. We share much of the same DNA, and like every living thing we exist in an unbroken chain stretching back across billions of years to a common ancestor – the first life on Earth. And Earth is dying.

Indeed, we are creating an extinction event comparable to that which occurred in the Cretaceous era when the dinosaurs died. That was what one might call a cosmic accident when an asteroid hit what was later to become the Gulf of Mexico. What we are doing through ignorance, greed, stupidity and indifference could equally be referred to as a cosmic crime - the destruction of life on a planetary scale. In fact, a criminal event of so great a magnitude that there is not a word for it in the English language. It is symptomatic of the contempt for Nature ingrained in our societies, exemplified by our institutionalized cruelty to animals whether in the laboratory or in the factory farm.

We do not have a false romantic view of Nature. Its beauty is equally matched by its cruelty and the life of almost every creature is "nasty brutish and short" with an unpleasant end awaiting the overwhelmingly vast majority. That is how Nature is, and that is right. Animals are adapted to their world and do not make moral choices, unlike us. Also unlike us they have no power to make it otherwise. However, it is a fact that this is their world as much as ours and we have no Right to either increase that suffering or dispossess them.

However, there is a utilitarian view for preserving life on Earth even apart from the potential dangers to Humanity of an ecological collapse. It is that the true treasure of this world is its genetic information. Every virus, microbe, plant and animal is the end result of billions of years of evolution. Each one of these is a unique development unlikely to be found anywhere else in the universe. When we destroy a species it is the equivalent of an illiterate savage burning down a library because it is more convenient to burn books than fetch firewood from outside the hut.

By the time we are capable of reading, fully understanding and utilizing the treasure-house of genetic information that is Earth most of it will have eradicated beyond hope of retrieval. What should be happening at the very least is to catalog all the species of life on Earth, so at least we are aware of what is being lost. Additionally, and most important, the genetic information of each species must be preserved, if possible along with details of its local environment and ecological niche. This is by no means a trivial program. It may cost as much in total as fighting a small war.

Finally, and perhaps in the far future if we fail now, the rich tapestry of life can be recreated by a saner society than exists today. Assuming that an advanced genetic engineering capability exists it will be possible for them to edit out defects that arise from what will have to be a limited gene pool, and reconstruct the ecology. This may not save those animals that have a culture that is imparted to their young, most notably the primates and cetaceans, but also including such animals as elephants. Trying to restart, say, a dolphin species purely from genetic information might be like aliens from another world tying to bring up a human child when they had no concept of language. However, it may be all that we have.

The Bright Green Future

Most contemporary people know what the term "Green" means in politics, or think they do. The Green parties around the world have as their primary aim the preservation of the natural world. However, no party can stand for election on a single issue, so consequently other policies have been grafted on. Unfortunately, one tendency has been that of the Luddite – a very strong antipathy to science and technology, even in some cases to the potential detriment of the environment. The Greens wish to move to a "sustainable" future, which is quite possible. However, there are two possible such futures. Apparently the preferred Green future is one of vastly lower population density, with very low energy consumption and a relatively static low technology global culture. The alternative is the Transhumanist vision, the so-called Bright Green alternative. This is also sustainable, but requires a high energy input probably from a mix of solar and nuclear power in order to support a higher population than today (currently 7 billion). The high energy input is needed for a far greater level of recycling, probably down to the atomic level, without significant pollution. This would be coupled with a shift in economic growth from large mass object such as cars to small intelligent devices and information. Food would also undergo a hitech transition to something like hydroponics or aeroponics, resulting in less land being used for cultivation than today.

In fact, it is worth exploring the limits to population density and food production, taking England as an example. Right now England is, at a push, capable of feeding its (approximate) population of 50 million from its own farmland. Notably, this is a population density of just under 400 per square kilometer. If we did a crude extrapolation to the total land area of the earth, some 150 million square kilometers, we could assume that the Earth could support around 60 billion and not be too unpleasantly overcrowded. However, the situation is even better than that if we look at hightech farming techniques such as hydroponics as a replacement for existing agriculture. The notion of plowing some dirt once a year, putting in a few seeds and leaving it all to the mercy of the weather really is a horribly crude and inefficient way of creating food. Even worse is how we use a lot of those crops to feed animals that we then slaughter for meat. So, let me present a Transhumanist vision of farming as it could be.

What do we need to grow crops? Well, in no particular order, sunlight, water, nutrients and labor. So, let's start where there is plenty of sunlight – the Sahara desert. Naturally, we have to pipe in the water which means almost immediate evaporation in conventional farming. Then let's do it in an enclosed environment, a kind of "super greenhouse". Now we can recycle the water lost this way. Let's also get out of the dirt, or more specifically sand. It's useless. Instead, we do it with hydroponics by feeding the crops the nutrients it needs directly with the crops being grown and supported on frames and in troughs. Finally, rather than staff it with vast numbers of workers, automate most of it with robots.

The energy to create the nutrients, fix atmospheric nitrogen and power the system as a whole comes from land dedicated to solar energy production, of which there is an abundance. So, how much can we expect? Well, there are commercial enterprises already in existence that can produce something like 250 tonnes of vegetables per hectare per year. That's enough to feed around 125 people for a year. Ten percent of the Sahara is around one million square kilometers. There are one hundred hectares per square kilometer so we could feed 125 x 100 x 1 million people, or in round numbers twice the current population of Earth. Existing farmland could be returned to Nature. Food is not a technological problem – it is a political one.

Nowhere can the difference between contemporary Greens and Bright Greens be seen as starkly as in the attitude towards the future of Earth. At one end of the Transhumanist spectrum are those who would like to see Earth abandoned by Humanity in the long term and it effectively become a garden. At the other are those who would engineer it in a massive way at the same time as we modify ourselves, and our intelligent machines, to integrate into it in a manner not before seen or previously contemplated – except as a recreation of the Garden of Eden.

Consider one vision of the future amongst many.
The world is reforested, the air is clean and from the orbital industries it appears almost uninhabited. However, some of the trees are quite different from any that have ever existed, because they are genetically engineered to be homes to a new kind of people. Their leaves photosynthesize with high efficiency, and the energy is converted eventually into electricity and food for the inhabitants. As for meat – they still eat it, but it does not come from animals. The waste of the people is absorbed into the roots of the tree, and when it rains the water is collected automatically and stored for later use. The people themselves seem remarkably technology free - because almost all of the planetary communications networks interface directly into their minds. All information, video, music, communication and so forth is theirs almost on a par with their own memories, and the bandwidth is such that it provides a fully immersive virtual reality, obviating most travel. Indeed, most of the life and business of the world is conducted in cyberspace, not the "real" world. Planet dwelling Humanity is diverse in ways it would be hard to imagine now – race, for example, is now a matter of choice and fashion. The people are healthy, the average intelligence engineered to be far higher than today's norm, and they age far more slowly than we do. They are also fully integrated with the biosphere, and the world is restored.

The End of Suffering

Love the animals: God has given them the rudiments of thought and joy untroubled.
Fyodor Dostoyevsky

The religion that most people associate with this notion is Buddhism and the Eightfold Way. As I mentioned in the introduction, there are a number of problems with this philosophy which have prevented it becoming an effective mass philosophy that actually delivers on its promise. The most obvious one is that it is simply too difficult for most people to follow to the required degree. Moreover, when suffering is the result of genetic predispositions resulting in various forms of mental illness it becomes almost impossible. There is however another drawback that could not have been anticipated by pre-modern people. It is that although supposedly applying to all sentient creatures the Eightfold Way is clearly not a recipe that can be followed by animals. The assumption of some sects that animals possess a soul that evolves through multiple incarnations into higher and higher lifeforms to the point where it can understand these teachings and thereby free itself from suffering is not tenable at face value. At the very least, the suffering continues even as I write and it will do so as long as life exists in its present form. So far that has been several hundred million years. This brings us to a proposal which is very modern, and is one of the Transhumanist answers, namely the Abolitionist Project as conceived by the philosopher David Pearce. This itself is a subset of what has come to be known as Paradise Engineering.

The basis of the projects rely on the surprising fact that the biology underlying suffering in most of its forms is relatively simple, and common across the vertebrate kingdom. Different levels of pain, both physical and psychological, do not affect people to the same degree. Everyone has different thresholds which are largely determined by a handful of gene variants, or alleles. In a few rare instances there are people who are born without the ability to feel pain at all, or are emotionally resilient to amazing degree. At the other extreme are those to whom the slightest injury results in intense pain, or in the psychological realm suffer from chronic depression or what amounts to post traumatic stress from relatively minor shocks (minor to most people, that is). This level of involuntary pain and suffering serves no purpose.

The suggestion is to use biotechnology to maximize happiness and minimize suffering. Superficially it appears modest. After all, we use anesthetics and analgesics to eliminate pain and antidepressants to alleviate mental suffering. However, when taken to its logical conclusion the ambitious scope of the project becomes apparent. It is nothing less than genetically re-engineering the entire biosphere to eliminate pain and suffering in all vertebrates in a Post-Darwinian transition that is a blueprint for:

- Rewriting the vertebrate genome
- Redesigning the global ecosystem
- Delivering genetically pre-programmed well-being

Of course, the means to do this are the various technologies expanded upon elsewhere. The initial impetus to act upon Nature this way comes from the way we ourselves (mis)treat animals. As I write some sixty *billion* animals are killed for food worldwide every year, quite often in appalling circumstances involving pain and suffering on a gigantic scale. Most people, of course, have a mental disconnect between what they buy from the supermarket and how the neatly packaged product gets there. It's an addiction, it's "natural" and it is not going away. That is one reason why many people choose a vegetarian lifestyle, but it is not sufficient. There are two other things that we can, and should do. The first is one advocated by the US animal rights organization PETA, which has recently offered a one million dollar prize to the first scientist to produce and bring to market in vitro meat. That is, real meat cultured from animal cells. The benefit would not only be to reduce the number of animals killed but also greatly reduce the environmental and feed costs associated with traditional farming. So far progress is modest, with many questions still to be resolved ranging from texture (does it look and feel like meat?) to taste (does it taste like meat?) to health issues that may arise in the manufacturing process. The most likely near term product may well be something akin to mincemeat, but if that replaced just a few percent of the meat in burgers it would save tens of millions of animals. There is also the "yuk factor" with the term "Frankenmeat" being coined for the product. Maybe one should compare it with the yuk factor of the screaming of animals in a slaughterhouse running with blood to get some real perspective. Needless to say, the amount spent on this research is a pittance compared to the subsidies farmers receive for raising animals.

The second approach to reducing the suffering of factory farmed animals is to either selectively breed, or more likely genetically engineer, farm animals so that they do not feel pain or stress to the degree to which they are currently susceptible. The fact that cloned animals have been approved for Human consumption may well make this task easier in that only a handful of such animals need serve as the template. Not to mention that most domesticated food animals have been massively genetically engineered already, albeit by selective breeding. Nevertheless, there are two obvious downsides. The first is simply the difficulty of getting current agribusiness to invest in reducing animal suffering in a manner that is more than pseudo-ethical window dressing. The other objection raised is that making animals more tolerant of cruel practices would encourage a relaxation of standards until we are back where we started. Alternatively it may alleviate some of the guilt associated with meat eating that might have resulted in a vegetarian or vegan lifestyle.

> *The wolf will live with the lamb, and the leopard will lie down with the young goat; The calf, the young lion, and the fattened calf together; and a little child will lead them.*
> Isaiah 11:6

Returning to "Nature red in tooth and claw" one can envisage a virus tailored for each species to tweak the genes governing pain and stress response to limit those responses when the animal meets its inevitably unpleasant demise. David Pearce would go even further and re-engineer the entire planetary ecosystem to remove predators and the "red in tooth and claw" bit completely, replacing them with vegetarian variants. The potential complexity of this proposal is daunting given that it would require a massive re-balancing of the ecosystem to limit population over-growth by methods other than death through starvation, disease and conflict. If this could be achieved through advanced Human or machine intelligence it would live up to the description of Paradise Engineering as the wolf really would lie down with the lamb in a world where pain and suffering have been replaced with peace and joy for all creatures. In the meantime we must face other decisions over the natural world.

Uplifting

Uplifting is a simple concept with major ethical ramifications. Do we have a right, or even a duty, to raise the intelligence of some species? So while a talking cat might seem really attractive to cat lovers, it may not be so much fun for the cat. Why, for example, would we stop at an intelligence that is subhuman, but an intelligence sufficient for it to recognize its own deformity? And if we do not stop at that point we certainly do not have something that can be described as a "cat". At best it would be a handicapped individual akin to an amputee, at worst a super predator as smart as we are. The problem is even more acute with monkeys and apes, and there would be a real risk of introducing a direct rival to Homo Sapiens, most especially if they were uplifted in order to provide a slave workforce – we have been down that road before with our own species, and it has not been a happy experience. On the other hand, why should we withhold increased intelligence from other animals who might benefit from it? The resolution to these questions is not clear-cut and is, in my opinion, one that should be left to the future and intelligences greater and wiser than ours.

But what of us in all of this?

Mirror Mirror...

Among the highest spiritual qualities one can certainly include such things as empathy and compassion. Indeed, compassion itself can probably be attributed to empathy, the ability to "feel" the joy or suffering of another and in some measure identify with them and their situation. This in turn leads to an active desire to alleviate the suffering of others and is one of the foundations of true love. It is one of the emotional facets that binds us not only to our fellow Humans but to all life in some degree or other.

So it is somewhat disturbing to discover that a minority of people do not have such feelings for their fellow creatures, lack a conscience and apparently feel no remorse or guilt for any of their actions. Usually termed *psychopaths* or *sociopaths*, the condition is described as *antisocial personality disorder*. These people make up an estimated one to four percent of the population and most of us have met one at some time or another. They are generally regarded as obnoxious, abusive, callous or hateful personalities. Unsurprisingly they make up a much larger percentage of the criminal population and can certainly be found amongst the most evil people in history.

The question is, how do such traits as empathy and conscience, guilt and shame arise in us? The answer would appear to be that we have in our heads an unconscious model of the world, ourselves and other people. We know instinctively how people are likely to react and we have an ideal image of ourselves that we would like to live up to (whether realistic or not). These models are created by our past experiences with the strongest being those forged in childhood. When our knowledge of who we really are, or what we have done, conflicts with this model it gives rise to feelings of failure manifest as guilt and shame. This is especially true if it involves a failure to match what we believe to be the expectation of other people as that also involves the "other people" model. Conscience is therefore the dissonance between what we are and what we would like to be, at least in terms of our actions and until we reconcile the two it troubles most of us. Similarly, empathy arises because the models we have of others are not passive things. The emulated emotions of the model are fed back to us resulting in shared sensations of feelings such as joy and sorrow. When these models are faulty or aspects of them are missing we end up with various disorders ranging from autism to narcissism to the aforementioned sociopathy. The result is, in general, a disconnect from the rest of society.

Returning to the nature of the sociopath, it is generally assumed it has both genetic and environmental causes. The latter very often includes a traumatic or abusive childhood or indeed, overt brain damage. However, most such childhoods do not result in an adult exhibiting such antisocial tendencies. Nor does possessing the necessary genetic background automatically result in a dysfunctional individual, at least as far as is known concerning the heritability of the condition. A combination of the two, however, is bad news.

Which brings us to the hard materialist interpretation these conditions – *mirror neurons*. These are a special type of braincell which have been found to fire both when an animal acts and when the animal observes the same action performed by another. Thus, the neuron "mirrors" the behavior of the other, as though the observer were itself acting. Such neurons have been directly observed in primates and other species including birds. In humans, such specialized activity has been found in the several areas of the brain.

It would appear that evolution has "hardwired" a spirituality into most if not all higher lifeforms. It appears to be most highly developed in Humans, who, despite all our failures do for the most part care not only about our fellows but have an expanded compassion that encompasses life and sentience in general. This is an especially important finding for two reasons. On one hand it may provide a therapeutic means of rectifying antisocial conditions or provide clues to treating the more extreme and debilitating forms of autism. On the other it may help save Humanity from future extinction caused by our own creations, most notably artificial intelligences. At least now we have a clue as to how compassion might be built into our future gods. We can envisage not only intelligences that dwarf our own, but a corresponding compassion that is so much greater than anything to which we might aspire. The poet Richard Brautigan named them in his 1967CE work: *All watched over by machines of loving grace.*

The PostHuman Condition

So far there has been talk about "PostHumans", but do we have any idea of what we may become? The brief and uninformative answer is "somewhere between what we are and Jupiter Brains". Nevertheless, it's fun to speculate a bit and extrapolate various trends from hard science, science fiction and fantasy. When we do so we find examples that again match elements of mythological creatures, both ancient and modern.

Probably the most conservative version of the PostHuman would look very much as we do now, with a few modifications, mostly internal. This would be the natural result of altering our genetics. We could, for example, envisage new versions of Humanity engineered to be far more disease resistant, impervious to aging, with the physical constitution of Olympic athletes and intelligence that would today be considered genius. Then there would be assorted "designer features" that would make race an arbitrary and alterable category. Perhaps we can catch a glimpse of the physical nature of such people in the Japanese manga depictions of such superhuman creatures, with their Elvish beauty. Or perhaps we have seen them for centuries as the Fae. A less pleasant model would be a mythological immortal creature of vast strength and speed, very hard to kill and which can morph between various forms from animals to something resembling a Utility Fog – the vampire. All of these would have a mind expanded by a direct access to external computational and information resources, including a planetary noosphere incorporating all animals and plants.

In the short term we might expect IQ boosts through nootropics ("smart" drugs) and life extension technologies to become commonplace, which is not really radical at all – just making people "better than well". Next step up would be the use of nanotech to modify our bodies and brains to a far higher degree of functionality. The gap opened up would be comparable to the one separating us from chimpanzees. At about the same time such technology would enable the uploading or transfer of minds into either simulated realities or synthetic bodies. The latter does unfortunately conjure images of big metal things full of electric motors clanking along, which is a long way from what would actually be possible. As we have seen, advanced nanotech is more akin to life than existing machinery and while some synthetic bodies would resemble the Human form they could be wildly different. In fact, there may be huge advantages in not sticking with the Human form but changing to something like the "fractal branching ultra-dexterous robots" proposed by Hans Moravec. These essentially consist of a central hub from which grow branches, or tentacles. Each of these subdivides into smaller branches and so on down to the nanometer scale with each being capable of independent movement. Not only does the furry version of Cthulhu have a full sensory input and locomotion from all its tentacles but it can manipulate matter down to the atomic level. In other words it can build anything it wants, including add-ons to itself, from almost any materials.

The ultimate in nanotech bodies would be ones that are totally reconfigurable and almost fluid, made from trillions of nanobots acting in a coordinated manner.

There is one more option often mentioned in connection with Transhumanism, which is the notion of the "Hive Mind" where individuals are subsumed into a collective mentality. In fiction the most notable example is the Borg of Star Trek fame where individuality is forcibly suppressed and people are coerced into joining via the forced implantation of brain computer interfaces. The results being unrealistically dramatic, ranging from a bad skin condition to having their limbs replaced with tools to an inability to speak properly. This is, of course, the preferred model for conspiracy theorists to focus upon. However, let's look at this option from a more sympathetic and realistic point of view of the individual who is about to voluntarily join.

First, there is unlikely to be any overt sign of membership of the hive mind. If anything voice, skin condition and general health will be significantly better than a normal Human. Unlike the Borg the members of the collective would probably be very attractive physically, extremely well spoken and definitely be able to communicate in a manner other than via threatening cliches. The subjective impression upon joining would be one of a massive expansion of consciousness, knowledge and memory where suddenly "I" am the collective. It would appear to be an incredible burgeoning of *individuality* and power where the individual would apparently "take over" the collective. So, what of "free will"? Well, you would still be able to exercise it just as when you were not a member of the hive mind. The difference is that now you would understand so much more that some of your previous beliefs and opinions would be shown as being either false or simply naive. What it most definitely would not be like is some external agency "possessing" you against your will in an almost demonic form and moving you like a badly choreographed puppet.

Piling on the speculation a bit, how would such a PostHuman mind arise? Well, as I write there are experiments designed to create an artificial electronic hippocampus. This is the part of the brain responsible for laying down and retrieving memories, and the work is ostensibly about creating prosthetics for those suffering from brain damage. However, what it would enable is computer access to this process as a first step to uploading, downloading and backing up memories. The question then arises as to what might happen if individuals wearing such a prosthesis were networked together so that they all had access to each others memories and knowledge. It may be that a collective superego might form – the prototype hive mind. After all, a large part of our personality, the notion of "who I am" undoubtedly resides with our memories of who we are and were. This is certainly the claim with a traditional belief in reincarnation where a person "remembers" their past lives. It might also be the logical endpoint of social networking on the Internet.

Which brings us to the mentality of the PostHuman condition in all its forms. The key aspect, irrespective of various boosted faculties, consciousness and senses must be control. That is, one's control over one's own mind. To understand what this means we need to look at the nature of our own mentalities. To do so we can either call upon modern psychology, or step back two and a half thousand years to the original analysis presented by the Buddha. This was before it accumulated the cultural baggage of the East with which many today associate it. Either view illuminates not "the" Mind, or even "the" Self, but many Minds and Selves that as a dynamic composite comprise the thing that is labeled as "me" (or you, for that matter). "I" change moment to moment as attention shifts, emotions come into play, the bodily cycles ebb and flow and all manner of thought and sensation, conscious and unconscious, flit about the brain. The Buddha summed it up in the Diamond Sutra, something I regard as one of the greatest religious and philosophical writings of all time:

> "...if there are beings who listening to this Sutra are able to believe, to understand, and to hold it, they will indeed be most wonderful

beings. Why? Because they will have no idea of an ego, of a person, of a being, or of a soul. For what reason? The idea of an ego is no-idea (of ego), the idea of a person, a being, or a soul is no-idea (of a person, a being, or a soul). For what reason? They are Buddhas who are free from all kinds of ideas... All composite things (samskrita) are like a dream, a phantasm, a bubble, and a shadow; are like a dew-drop and a flash of lightning; They are thus to be regarded."

The modern view is perhaps best summarized by the following quote from Minsky's book *Society of Mind*:

"What magical trick makes us intelligent? The trick is that there is no trick. The power of intelligence stems from our vast diversity, not from any single, perfect principle. Our species has evolved many effective although imperfect methods, and each of us individually develops more on our own. Eventually, very few of our actions and decisions come to depend on any single mechanism. Instead, they emerge from conflicts and negotiations among societies of processes that constantly challenge one another."

That is, the Human mind is a gestalt which is defined as:

"...a physical, biological, psychological, or symbolic configuration or pattern of elements so unified as a whole that its properties cannot be derived from a simple summation of its parts."

It is now generally accepted that the thing that calls itself "Me" or "I", the Ego is not something that is in control - it just thinks it is. It is more akin to a self-referencing label attached to the Mind/Body composite. Experiments have shown that even when a person believes that "they" make a particular decision, even so simple a one as to raise a hand, the brainwaves (evoked potentials) show that the decision is actually executed up to a second before the ego claims it decided.

The reality is that we are Legion. The question then becomes what happens when "we" do not march in step, or even in the same direction? The last example of the above offers the clue. The mind divided against itself is weak. One part is obstructing the other, which at best results in a certain degree of indecision. After all, how often are people "in two minds" about something? At worst, the division is manifested in the body as opposing facets compete. The results are stress and disease (dis-ease) of mind and body, because the reality is that they are a physical unity. The person feels ill at ease, there is suffering that no simple quick course of action will alleviate. To paraphrase an old saying, you cannot please all of the facets all of the time if they are in competition. It is the modern neurological picture partially underlying the Buddhist notion of Suffering. In many instances, it is a case of "wants" vying with "needs" and "oughts". We know what we ought to do, what we need to do and what we want... and all of these might be pulling us in different directions.

The truth of the matter is encoded into English and other Germanic languages in our everyday speech, yet passes generally unrecognized by most people. If our Mind is not integrated, we lack Integrity. If it is not whole, we are not Holy. The latter word is derived from the Indo-European root hailo- or kailo- "free from injury, whole", whence comes also English hale as in "hale and hearty". There are cognates in the Germanic languages, for example German heilig, Swedish helig "holy".

The divided mind is weakness incarnate. It can be pushed and pulled in many different and conflicting directions with ease, and because this is so, it cannot be predicted or trusted. It is one of the major sources of unease that people experience around some types of the mentally ill and around those people who are fickle, "shallow", "self" centered or totally untrustworthy. There is no placid depth to the ocean of mind, only churning foam with tides running in all directions. It is why the pre-eminent Christian prayer requests of God "...lead us not into temptation..." Real temptation is a "regret if you do, regret if you don't" situation. It is a situation that forces a division of the Mind. That's why it is temptation, after all, and why it should be avoided.

How someone arrives in such a state is a matter for debate along the usual lines of Nature/Nurture, but the Mind can be trained. Again, the methods for disciplining the mind are millennia old. Pavlov, the Behaviorists, Conditioned Reflex etc are all old discoveries. The key to any kind of training is repetition and reinforcement. Tendencies, which are themselves mind fragments, get stronger and more deeply entrenched through practice and use, and fade away with disuse. It is, in fact, why discipline is a virtue, and also lies at the heart of the Buddhist Eightfold Way. If there is no self-discipline the mind simply becomes a jungle. The discipline is exerted in a particular direction with some tendencies being exercised, and some excised by being allowed to wither and die, almost as if one were cultivating a garden. The overall framework that we use for setting a direction for the Society of Mind must be consistent. It is called ethics when it is applied to our interaction with others, and self discipline when applied to ourselves. The methods used fall under many names, meditation and prayer being the two most commonly associated with religious practice, although such practices do not have to be formal or even recognized for what they are. But what if we did not need to cultivate that discipline? What if it came naturally to a mind that was not divided in such a way?

The best way to examine this is to imagine what it would be like for an ordinary person to have this kind of superhuman control and integration of mind. Probably the most noticeable thing would be that whatever you decided to do would be interesting and emotionally rewarding. That includes necessary household chores and other mundane and boring necessities. If you wanted to learn something, no matter how difficult or dry the subject, it would fascinate you. You would not have to force yourself, with one eye on the clock and periods of daydreaming about what you are going to do when the tedious study session is over. You would have full control over your emotional states and when faced with temptation where there are two desirable yet exclusive options to choose from, you would choose and be able to put the path not taken aside with no regrets or remorse. Indeed, levels of pleasure and pain themselves would be under conscious control. Your willpower would effectively be infinite as would your ability to focus on any task you felt necessary. Love and hate could be summoned or banished at will, as could jealousy and possessiveness. You could not be coerced, threatened or tortured. Fear could be banished instantly, including fear of death.

This does however imply a higher level goal seeking directive. What this means is that there must be something that chooses what we would become, since if we can be anything mentally where does the initial impetus come from? In contemporary Humanity our primal "programming" is through Nature and is closely tied with survival and reproduction. It is these two factors that underlie much of what we want, and do, even if buried deep under the lifetime of social conditioning to which most of us are subject. Sex, survival and death are of course some of the great themes of psychology and psychiatry, but what happens when they no longer have the power to shape us?

Initially, for those making the transition to PostHuman the old instincts will determine and constrain the first great changes of mentality. However, when those instincts are themselves removed and replaced by others we can only guess. Maybe when there is no deep fear of death and extinction it will suddenly seem rational to embrace cessation or non-existence. Or maybe not. It may largely depend on the truth behind the reality of our situation in the multiverse, and those intelligences as yet beyond us.

What sort of society would result from that, where everyone is effectively what would now be regarded as an incorruptible fanatic or a saint? I have no idea, but it would be radically different from what we have now which is driven by combinations of fear, greed and stupidity being held at bay by love, altruism and intelligence. Indeed, we have no idea where the existing world is going if nothing changes, but it is likely to be bad based on our historical track record.

Can we do better than try and imagine what being suddenly uplifted to a PostHuman mentality might *feel* like? Well, it is impossible to know for sure, but one clue is the expanded consciousness created by the psychedelic drugs like LSD. With these one perceives directly the vast raw information flows from the senses and internal aspects of our mind as they communicate with each other. The barrier between conscious and unconscious is removed along with their censors and filters and raw reality floods in. In dreams the most ridiculous things seem to make sense because our higher brain functions are switched off. Similarly when we expand our consciousness much of this waking world looks decidedly implausible, and we see that many of the things we thought logical and obvious make no real sense at all in the light of our new perceptions. Psychedelic drugs have that effect in that they give us perceptions more akin to a superhuman mind. The problem, of course, is that although these might be very similar to a PostHuman information flow into the conscious mind we do not, as Humans, have the raw processing power or intelligence to handle it.

Anyway, whatever happens, it may well be all or none of the above or simply be beyond our imagination. That is, after all, the nature of the Singularity.

To end this section, the opponents of Transhumanism often claim that it either denies, or intends to destroy, our "humanity". The truth is exactly the opposite. We seek to voluntarily extend everything that makes us Human in the first place. That is, all the qualities that distinguish us from other animals. Our critics unspoken assumption as to what "humanity" entails are usually a catalog of Human frailties and failings – the very stuff of dramatic novels. For example: greed, jealousy, stupidity, ignorance, cruelty, pain, suffering and death. They define humanity by its worst characteristics and ailments, not its best. By doing so they also implicitly condone coercion since much of the above, and its consequences like war, crime and starvation, are not some kind of sport played only by consenting adults.

Dreams of Brahma

The uncreated Hindu God Brahma sleeps and dreams the universe into existence. When he awakes, the universe is destroyed, only to be recreated when he returns once more to sleep.

Am I a man who dreamed of being a butterfly, or am I a butterfly dreaming that I am a man? - Chuang Tzu

or

Am I a man who dreams of being a God, or a God who dreams of being a man?

One of the great comforts of traditional religions has been their doctrine of eternal life. That is, the notion that the death of loved ones is not the end and that they continue to survive in (hopefully) a better place. That after death a reunion is possible in an afterlife. It may be true, it will be true.

Even now simulated realities are a big business with games constantly taking advantage of the latest increases in computing power to render ever more realistic environments, and Hollywood using supercomputers to create photo-realistic special effects. It will not be too long before the simulation one sees on a screen is indistinguishable from a camera pointed at a real scene, and the game will also implement physical laws and so behave like the real world. If one were to drop an emulated Human mind into that environment it may well be impossible for it to discover that it was not in the "real" reality, especially if it was surrounded by other Human, or Human level, intellects.

Bearing this in mind, the *Simulation Argument* runs something like this. One part of this trilemma must be true:

- We will never reach a technological level capable of producing simulated realities.
- Even if we can do so, we never will.
- We are probably living in a simulation.

More simply stated, if someone somewhere sometime is running real-world simulations what are the chances that this reality, where I am writing this and you are reading it, is one of them? The answer depends purely on the number of such simulations. If there are none, ever, then what we see around us is certainly real. If a million such simulations are run over the lifetime of the universe, the chances of this being the real world is a *million to one* against. The real number might well be far in excess of a million eventually – maybe even in the trillions over the coming centuries or millennia. One possible indicator of the numbers might be if our near term descendants wanted to bring back their deceased loved ones via such a simulation. If this was possible by the end of the century, with a world population of around ten billion and each returning just their parents and grandparents, the number would be in the tens of billions.

There is a particular image conjured up in the mind when reading about realities simulated on a computer, namely that of someone sitting at a futuristic PC simulating a universe like a video game. This will most definitely *not* be the case. It is ludicrous for the simple reason that the computer itself will likely be vastly smarter than any Human alive today. There is not going to be a future where you pop down to the local computer store and buy one of those for the kids, or to do your word processing and browse the Net. Long before that point has arisen we will have either merged with our technology and achieved some kind of apotheosis or simply been superseded by it and have become extinct. The only get-out would be if such simulations will never, ever, happen and the only (im)plausible reason would be if the Human mind could not be run on a computer of any type, even a synthetic biological one. Nor will computers remain the kind of primitive boxes we see around us now. As we have seen, they will be as ubiquitous as life itself, blending into and perhaps forming part of everything from our homes and machines to our own minds to a part of every blade of grass and every leaf on every tree. The natural world will merge with the synthetic to create a global mind, Gaia, whose intellect will be trillions of times greater than that of any Human now alive and in which the vast majority of Humanity in its various forms will spend most of their conscious lives. We see the beginnings of the Goddess now, in the Internet as it becomes the world's nervous system and to which more and more work and play migrates.

So we need a word that more accurately conveys the feeling and reality of our experience of the world around us. "Simulation" or "emulation" sounds clinical, cold and mentally distances the us from intuitively connecting the concept with mundane existence as we all perceive it. So, following on from the Brahmic dream analogy we will borrow a word from the Advaita Vedanta philosophy – Maya. The concept of Maya was introduced by the great 9th Century Hindu philosopher Adi Shankara and refers to the limited, purely physical and mental reality in which our everyday consciousness has become entangled. It is held to be an illusion and a veiling of the true, unitary self. So we are almost certainly living in a world of Maya, probably one of many levels of Maya. Clearly, the idea that this world is not the real one has a lot of history behind it and is far from new, cropping up as it does in various Eastern religions as well as Gnosticism in the West. What is new is the insight that science may provide into the mechanism underlying this notion.

We would also like to give a generic name to whoever or whatever is generating the Maya in its various forms and levels. Some may be PostHumans, or machine intelligences or genuine extraterrestrial aliens or perhaps something we cannot imagine. Collectively, we are going to call them the Shen. This is a word used in Chinese religion and philosophy which has many meanings, generally revolving around the notion of deities and spirits. So collectively the Shen would include all of the possible causative agents listed above, including those we might also call angels and gods. Two questions then arise – who or what is responsible, and why? To examine the possibilities further we need to decide the type of world in which we are living.

If this world is not baseline reality, where are we? There are a number of possible alternatives each increasing in complexity. Furthermore it may be that we have something very much akin to the esoteric notion of different planes of reality. All we can say for certain is that if this is so, we are at the very bottom as far as Human level intelligence is concerned. So let's take the possibilities in terms of ascending order.

Given that we can emulate a brain, then feeding it with realistic sensory data from other emulated brains via a simulated world would be a relatively simple task. For example there is no need to simulate the interior of a tree until that tree is cut down and somebody takes a look at it. Ditto the center of the Earth or the surface features of Neptune. This is slightly more complex than the "brain in a jar" scenario of the movie *The Matrix* where Humans live out their lives in a simulated world by having their bodily sensory inputs hijacked by a computer and fed false, but consistent, data. Interestingly, the existence of psychedelics drugs would seem to rule out such a straightforward situation where the brain is real but the world an illusion as it would not be possible to easily mimic the psychedelia. It does however suggest that maybe the world around us is not as detailed as we might suppose, and that things only exist in detail when we look for them. There is no reason why this would not include the insides of our bodies, or even our brains! In fact, our bodies may have no direct relationship to our minds, except indirectly via the Maya.

The lowest level that could generate the world we see around us is that created by a single Shen of PostHuman power, probably in our near future, with a mental capacity exceeding ours as we exceed that of a bird. It may not even be deliberate. Even now, we constantly run simulations in our own heads, for example we imagine things like "what will happen if I turn up for work late?" by running through the scenario complete with models of the people involved acting as we expect they might. A Shen speculating, or remembering, what it was like to live in these times may well create the level of detail we see in the world around us. In this case almost certainly the entity is you, after you have been augmented, and the likely time period is within this century. So the real date is possibly something like 2111CE, and not 2011CE as I write this. This is obviously more likely if you are young (in this world), and less so if you are old. Here is a riddle:

> If I determine that when I am PostHuman I will run what-if scenarios of my past life, does that make it more likely that I am living in one of those simulations? The answer is "Yes" - but only if this is the real world!

Why would you do this? One possible reason would be curiosity, to see how your life would have played out had certain paths been followed. We can all remember crucial incidents or decisions where our life could have taken an entirely different direction. As a demigod we could get to determine what kind of person we might have become, and summing across all these possible lives we would really know our True Self under many more varied circumstances than a single Human lifetime could encompass. What would you be like now had you chosen to marry X instead of Y? If you had children, or no children? And these are just the big choices. How much hinges on chance, and how much on personality? If it takes a lifetime to know "your face before you were born" as the Buddhists riddle goes, how many more lives does it take to know all that you could have been? That's not to say that all this happens sequentially as one conventionally might assume with the notion of reincarnation. It could all happen simultaneously in a Great Mind, the result being that we live "parallel lives". Perhaps one day you might have a particularly vivid dream of another life, yours but not yours…

Or perhaps sleep and dreams are still necessary for demigods, and this is a dream of perfect detail. I know that I occasionally have lucid dreams, where I am conscious within the dream that it is unreal. On one occasion I knelt down and looked at the dream grass and was amazed by the level of realism and detail. How much more perfect would an intellect vastly greater than Human create it? Of course, dreams are betrayed by their own crazy logic or lack of it. This is often one of the triggers for entering a lucid phase. In my case, it's flying. As soon as I fly in a dream I know it's a dream, but until then even quite bizarre events seen normal, such as cats talking! Upon waking, however, the illogical nature of the state (my own Maya) becomes apparent. Maybe when our Shen self wakes the illogical nature of what we think of as our normal waking reality is readily apparent. I mean, does this world around us *really* make sense, with its pointless cruelty, pain, suffering, stupidity and ignorance played out on a beautiful planet where all of it is self inflicted?

This is Solipsism – the notion that only "I" exist and that everything around me is a figment of my imagination. That everything I see around me is Mind creating a theory to explain its own existence. Of course, there has to be a certain degree of amnesia because I cannot actually remember that this is so, although various meditative techniques or drugs can open my mind to that particular reality. There is even a word to describe the condition of such recall – *anamnesis*, and it lies at the heart of the Neo-Gnostic worldview.

However, a solipsistic Maya is the cheapest in terms of Mind. In other words, only one thing is being created in any detail, and that is you. If this is so, where does that leave other people? It rather implies that the vast bulk of Humanity consists of what the games world calls NPCs, or "non player characters" . They do not have to be resolved in any detail whatsoever except as they interact with you, being essentially figments of the dreamworld. At the lowest level they would be only be playing their scripted role. For example, it does not require much for them to say things like: "Do you want fries with that?" when ordering food from one of them. Even less so if you are the one asking that question of a customer! At a higher level, with friends and family, close proximity and detailed interaction may raise them to the level of full consciousness, at least in your presence in order to maintain the illusion. Additionally, most of the world will not exist in any detail except as you move through it. What happens when you are not around would be some kind of superficial evolution of gross features almost like a soap opera on TV, with a basic script being worked through. This would be applied to both people you never meet and geography. Was there recently really a hurricane that flooded New Orleans? So I hear, but it would not be any more than that unless I went there, whereupon the correct level of damage would be filled in for me to view, and the NPCs would tell me their scripted stories. So you are the lead character in your own dream, with a consciousness reduced from, but still part of, your True (or Higher) Self. When the dream ends you will awaken into a new reality. Having said all this, there are some general rules that it is foolish to ignore. If we jump off a tall building we will break our bones, and if we treat the people around us badly we will reap the consequences of our actions, and one thing we can be absolutely sure of is that pain hurts. When we dream this world without true consciousness it runs like clockwork with rigid rules. When we open our consciousness to encompass those around us as part of our True Self we can do anything. Even, perhaps, wake up and dream this reality lucidly.

Speaking of which, how might one awake and return to the real world? It has been speculated that there might be hidden codes one could utter, like spells, in order to shut down the program or remove oneself from it. Clearly, speaking the words "End the simulation!" does not work and it cannot be something so obvious. Or can it? Perhaps every one of us already knows the exit code – we call it *death*. However, before you hang, shoot or poison yourself in order to exit a particularly nasty bit of what you believe to be simulated reality, ask yourself this: "Why am I here in the first place, given that I would have inevitably known such a state was not only possible but likely?" Pushing the exit button may well simply result in a "Fail" and you might be forced to resit the exam. Again. Alternatively, allow it to run its course to one of two possible endings. The first is, as mentioned, death. In which case it would be just like waking up in the morning from a particularly vivid dream. The second is more radical, which is to get out alive by riding the wave of Maya to the Apocalypse where our consciousness expands and merges with the True Self. This latter resolution is the preferred method of the Praxis, not least because it avoids the unpleasantness of the dying experiencing.

Going up a level would bring us to a Maya created by a group of Shen within something like the Gaian Mind. The major difference being that most, if not all, of the people around us are real and not figments of our expanded imagination. Beyond that would lie the Mind of Gaia Herself, as far beyond Human intellect as we are beyond an earthworm. Further levels of reality may exist above even this. For example, consider the *Fermi Paradox*, also known as *The Great Silence*. Simply stated, this is the question posed about intelligent life in the universe, namely, why do we not see any? No radio or laser signals, no spacecraft and especially no cosmic engineering as far as we can see, which is billions of light years out into space and back in time. What can we deduce from this? Maybe intelligent life is incredibly rare and we are alone in the vastness. Or nobody ever, over billions of years and trillions of trillions of stars, indulges in cosmic engineering or expansion. Or perhaps, keeping with our Neo-Gnostic theme, we do not live in the real universe at all.

Consider the notion that the first civilization to arise, whom we shall call the *Progenitors*, expands to effectively implement a Transhumanist agenda and initially stripmines its own galaxy and then the entire visible universe which it converts to Computronium. Bear in mind that this could have happened billions of years ago. Clearly such an act would curtail the evolution of life throughout the universe and certainly block naturally arising intelligence. From the Progenitor's point of view this in itself might be considered a great material loss as well as being unethical. So, how can they both have their cake and eat it? The answer is to run every planet they convert into Computronium in a simulation, most probably "on site" in a small corner of the Computronium that was made from the planet. Evolution would then proceed normally, or at least as normally as could be expected, in the Maya. Life would arise, then possibly intelligence. And if it followed the same route it would expand through its simulated universe converting all resources and recapitulating the steps of the Progenitors. However, there would be a number of differences.

The first, and most obvious, would be that only the target planet and its local environs would be rendered in any detail. In other words, from the inside it would look like there is only one civilization per universe. The inhabitants would ponder the Fermi Paradox.

The second is that as soon as they started converting the matter in their locale into Mind they would suddenly hit a metaphorical brick wall. The matter in their universe is only coarsely rendered and the Maya itself would be limited by the amount of Mind allocated by the Progenitors in the real world, which would be vastly less than the apparent bulk of the planet, let alone the visible universe. Indeed, it might only amount to a few tonnes. The result would be that as the inhabitants created their own Artilects or became PostHuman the whole facade would break down. At which point one of two things would happen. Either the Progenitors those people at all. This may have been because the method of reconstruction was not precise in this world. In which case... it makes no difference to us. We are who we are no matter what reality we inhabit. It's a strange world.

Finally, the question arises of whether we should resurrect the dead. Some might not wish to go through this process, nor be brought back. In some ways those who have expressed religious beliefs are the easiest to second guess. One does not sign up for (say) Christianity in the hope of staying dead, since a major part of its attraction is moving on to a better life in Heaven. Contemporary atheists, or those who have expressed no preferences, are another matter. So, if you do *not* wish to live again in such circumstances you should make a note of that somewhere. It would then become the post-death equivalent of a medical "Do Not Revive" notice.

Cartesian Dualism

One other problem the Simulation Argument might resolve, at this level at least, is whether or not the mind and body are in some way separate. In the philosophy of mind this Dualism is closely associated with the philosophy of René Descartes, which holds that the mind in the form of consciousness and self awareness, is a nonphysical "thing" distinct from the brain. Crudely put, does the consciousness arise from the brain or is the brain some kind of receiver for consciousness? Contemporary science very strongly favors the former hypothesis. However, if we are not in the baseline reality then it is quite possible our minds are generated elsewhere and our bodies are in fact a very convincing illusion.

Doomsday...

Finally, there is one other reason to suppose that the world we see around us is not the true one.

Suppose someone presented you with a bag of marbles and claimed that they contained a million blacks and one white, and then asked you to put your hand in and pick one of them. Which, of course, you do and amazingly you discover that it is white. Now this is an incredible piece of luck akin to winning the national lottery – in fact, a million to one probability. Then the person tells you that they have lied about the number of black marbles in the bag, although they do not actually tell you would terminate the Maya, or they would invite the new civilization to enter the real world. In other words, there would be an unveiling, or revelation, of the true nature of reality. In a literal etymological sense it would be the Apocalypse.

Nevertheless, before this stage is reached there would be a brief intermediate state where a PostHuman civilization of modest means would be feasible. At our present rate of progress it would likely last somewhere between a century and a millennium. During this period we could expect to possess sufficient power to create a deep Maya of our own.

Before examining the remaining options there is one other question we might ask – how long has this Maya been running? Actually, it is two questions since the rate of time flow in the real world would almost certainly be different from that here. As for how long this is from an internal point of view, it is impossible to say. It could potentially be billions of years, or only a few months, days or seconds. We have no way of knowing. To give some idea of the capacity of an ultimate computer consider the limit of a totally efficient computer of a few kilograms mass converting itself to energy in the process. It could generate a Maya encompassing the full lives of every Human being for the past ten thousand years in less than a millionth of a second. Then again, maybe all of history has not been simulated. Perhaps merely the past century, or just the time since I was born. Or maybe only the past few minutes of subjective time, with all my memories of childhood and what I had for breakfast yesterday created in situ as a perfect illusion (known as *The Omphalos Hypothesis* or more disparagingly *Last Thursdayism*). There are all sorts of weird possibilities.

There may even be levels above that of the hypothetical Progenitors. In his book *The Physics of Immortality* the physicist Frank Tipler speculates that in the last infinitesimally tiny fraction of a second within a collapsing universe there is infinite computing capacity released and that this constitutes baseline reality under the control of an infinite omniscient omnipotent intelligence. In a word – God. A God which is the endpoint of the evolution of life in a universe.

And speaking of universes, there are a number of peculiar consequences when one mixes notions of the multiverse with the Simulation Argument. If you recall, the notion of immortality arises in the multiverse because the spirit of a person is spread across multiple bodies so that if one body dies the spirit continues in the body that does not die. At worst, there is a lingering consciousness until something seemingly comes along to revive the person to full life. However, what happens in ancient history where there was no hope of miraculous technology? To take one pointed example, what happens to someone being guillotined during the French revolutionary period? The blade comes down, it slices through your neck and the last thing you see is the world rotating as your head falls into the basket. How do you get out of that one? Well, if this happened in the real universe rather than the Maya that might well be tricky. However, the multiverse is a big place both in spacial and temporal terms. The key is that somewhere, sometime, exactly the same thing will be happening in the Maya and you will awaken into some kind of afterlife. So not only do you migrate across the multiverse but your spirit effectively travels in time as well. So you may be killed in "reality" and migrate to the Maya. This is, of course, the scenario where the Shen resurrect the dead of past ages. You move from a Godless universe directly to the mind of a God.

From the Deep Past to Far Future

> *That is not dead which can eternal lie*
> *And with strange aeons even death may die*
> H P Lovecraft

There are other possible methods of bringing the long departed back to life that do not depend upon any special preparation of the body and which may be applicable to the dead in times past. However, they are technologies we can only vaguely glimpse from our Human perspective and is likely to be the kind of thing only something radically PostHuman could accomplish, or even understand.

The first is Quantum Archeology. The idea itself is fairly simple, namely that it seems that in our universe no information is actually lost since it is a conserved quantity like energy. So the details of everything, everywhere and everywhen might be regathered and reconstructed. As to how and where such information might be found there are only the vaguest speculations, such as mining the Event Horizons of Black Holes for all the information that has fallen into them and been captured. So the dead of ages past may be resurrected to live on, probably within the simulation spaces of something like a Matrioshka Brain – the mind of a God. This is no way to be considered some kind of second class existence since our physical reality will be a desperately poor place compared to the vast flows of information within such a brain. Indeed, the vast bulk of "stuff happening" in the universe will be in those worlds of thought.

Another possible method would be scanning across the multiverse to places where time has "frozen" and locating the point of death of the person in question before capturing their spirit. At present science says this is not possible, but that may not be the last word on the matter since we have no comprehensive theory linking the very small (Quantum Mechanics) with the very large (Cosmology and General Relativity).

Alternatively, some people have suggested that such archeology might really be incredibly simple, at least in principle, by applying enormous computational resources to contemporary social media sites and other records of a person's life. The idea itself is that their full mental state, and hence spirit, could be reconstructed from the kind of comments they make and the time they make them, coupled with contextual information ranging from contemporary news reports, photos, and history to DNA and medical records. The more details the more accurate the recreation of that person. One major problem is that calculations suggest that the records we leave behind are less than one thousandth of what is necessary, at best, to home in on a unique spirit that exactly matches the original. This is where the multiverse can "rescue" the situation because part of the reconstruction process can randomly guess what should fill the information gaps. The result of making that random guess is a spread of possible versions of the deceased across the multiverse, including at least one that exactly matches the original.

However, if you want to hedge your bets then get blogging and spread your thoughts and opinions around the Net, for while the meek may or may not inherit the Earth the loud mouthed and opinionated (or a close facsimile thereof) stand to inherit the cosmic future.

Somewhat more seriously, it may well also be possible to reconstruct a personality from the memories of those who knew the deceased, especially those who pass through the Apocalypse to acquire PostHuman status. For example, I have a record and model in my head of my dead parents. How they spoke, their interests, reactions and so forth. Combining that with DNA, photos, medical records, recollections of friends and so forth, if I had the power I could construct a replica of them that would be sufficiently detailed to fool me, or anyone else for that matter. Or, perhaps I am a reconstruction of Dirk Bruere (the original) put together by those who knew me and are children as I write this. In order to get an almost perfect replication of the original spirit they would need to hone me in a simulation where every major detail of my past life has been reconstructed, with one of the final tests being me writing these precise words at this precise time. In other words, my whole life has been scripted in order to recreate me, which is an interesting comment on fate and free will, at least up to a point. Have you ever made a life changing decision that you knew was obviously "wrong", even as you made it, and wondered why? I do not mean some big, well considered action but something trivial which later turned out to be an event that, had it gone differently, might have changed your life? If so this would be typical of a simulation designed to reconstruct you according to a detailed plan. Such an event would represent an overriding of your "free will" in favor of a script. After all, a slip of the tongue or an out of character spur of the moment decision would be far easier to engineer than a replay where you get to "choose" the correct (original) path. Assuming this is so (and I believe something like this really is true), how do I feel? Well, I am who I am and as far as I am concerned I must play the hand I have been dealt – as must we all.

This raises another question – what happens here when I exceed the lifespan of the original Dirk? The obvious answer is that, like the original, I die to the world - and then awake in the real one. Alternatively, I continue for some unspecified time in this one in order to accomplish what I did not manage first time around. Which begs another question, what of children who die young, or babies? This is in fact a variant of an old Christian theological problem concerning the destination of the souls of unbaptized infants who are too young to have committed personal sins but have not been absolved of the burden of Original Sin. The most well known hypothesis is that they go to Limbo, which is a state of either maximal happiness or minimal punishment, depending upon ones views. In fact, in Roman Catholic theology the question has never been definitively answered, especially as to whether the soul has any hope of finally attaining Heaven. In our version, resurrection would not be any different than for an adult, although before resurrection into the true reality they may be tested by allowing them to live the life they missed in this one.

If we are serious about the possibility of an agent from the future resurrecting us by a process as yet unknown it makes sense to at least give it as much help as possible, in both locating and identifying us. This means having records of our thoughts, actions, friends and so forth placed into a time capsule of sorts that may survive the Apocalypse or Singularity. At present the best medium, and the one most likely to evolve into planetary consciousness, is the Net. Additionally, for those deceased, an accurate time, date and place of death would no doubt be of use to Gaia, as would additional "Waypoints". These are times and places where our presence is recorded as having taken place. Consider it an aid to tracking us from the future. These can be simple observations such as... "Today, at 19.53 on 20 April 2011 I sat at my computer upstairs in my house", or can be both more complex and a lot more fun. Pilgrimages, of a sort where we go either alone or with a small group to somewhere notable, devoid of other people, and have a party doubling as a Sacrament! Again recording time and place on the Net (Twitter? - if it still exists, or a blog). We also need to extending this process backwards in time to our ancestors if possible, which is where such projects as the Mormon genealogical research is immensely valuable. The Church of Latter Day Saints (LDS) maintains the largest genealogy library in the world located in Salt Lake City, Utah, USA where more than two million rolls of microfilm are securely stored in the Granite Mountain Records Vault. The Church itself keeps records of infant blessings, baptisms, confirmations, marriages, and deaths (what we are calling Waypoints). From its beginnings, the Church has encouraged members to keep individual records – and we should do likewise. This includes keeping a diary of our mundane thoughts and experiences, plus the time of each diary entry. Finally, there is one more record that would be invaluable – a sample of our genetic structure. At present a full genome scan is prohibitively expensive, but an actual DNA sample should suffice. The simplest is somewhat traditional – a hair locket containing a sample of hair complete with follicle. Although not so common nowadays, it used to be a gift to a loved one, and may become so again for the reasons listed above.

A more modern variant would be to include an encased blood sample. Blood vial jewelery is easily available over the Net as part of the Vampire/Goth subculture. Of course, going the whole way, if one were to join a formal organization as discussed later we now have the reason why signing the membership document or contract in your own blood might me a good idea!

It may also be the case that the originals of ourselves, you and me, died long ago and we do not share exactly the same spirit and hence are not what the real number might be. So, you start thinking... how many black marbles are likely to be in the bag – what's a plausible number? One hundred perhaps? But picking a white marble from that would still be a one in a hundred chance. So perhaps ten might be more plausible, or even less.

Anyway, let's cut to a completely different scenario drawn from a science fiction view of the future of Humanity made popular in series like Star Trek, movies like Star Wars or any number of books over the past century. This is the one where we go on to populate the galaxy, and indeed universe, across millions of worlds and with trillions of trillions of Humans living and dying across millions of years. Now suppose we take a rather New Age view of a soul floating around in hyperspace or wherever souls waiting to incarnate reside, looking to randomly incarnate in a Human body located somewhere in space and time. So, it does this and discovers that it is now living on Earth in the early 21st Century. Amazing! Out of all those planets and all those times it could have found itself here it is, right at the very beginning when all of this was about to start. In fact, it is even more amazing than picking one white marble from a million black ones by choosing at random. And an uneasy thought arises – perhaps our assumption about the possible choices is wrong just like it was about the bag we first thought contained a million black marbles. What would that mean – that there is no science fiction future for Humanity?

Then let's consider the alternative future where Humanity becomes extinct fairly soon. Now when we look at the probability of existing here and now it becomes extremely high, because there is no tomorrow and most of the people who will ever live are around right now. The world we see is no longer extremely improbable at all. Therefore the statistics strongly suggest that Humanity does not have much time left and there is no galaxy spanning future. The immediate and obvious reply is that *someone* has to be first, which is true. It's just that it seems incredibly strange and improbable that we exist here and now since it is a *very* privileged position. Unless, of course, we are not where we think we are...

Theodicy

Be the change you want to see in the world
Gandhi

In the philosophy of religion and theology the problem of evil is the problem of reconciling the existence of evil or suffering in the world with the existence of an omniscient, omnipotent, omni-benevolent god or gods. A proposed solution to this dilemma is called a *theodicy*.

Before we jump into discussions about evil it is best if we define what we mean by evil. Most people think they know and are quite able to give examples such as child abuse or the murder of innocent people, from which it is easy to deduce that in these cases evil is the infliction of unnecessary pain and suffering, and by implication the person inflicting it is evil. The problem arises with the word "unnecessary", since no doubt famous mass murderers such as Stalin or Hitler would argue that what they did *was* necessary. Even serial killers can claim that their evil is necessary in order to gain personal pleasure from the suffering of their victims. Clearly then evil is a social relationship, since it would be impossible for a lone person to be, or do, evil if there is no sentient life for them to interact with.

Irrespective of the definition of evil acts, whether a person who commits them is evil per se is a moot point. Almost all legal systems recognize that normally good people can commit evil, and that the insane or brain damaged are not responsible for their actions. To be an evil person requires a knowledge of right and wrong and to deliberately choose such a path. Even then, such definitions are socially defined. However, a common theme involves lack of empathy or consideration for others and the Buddhist explanation is simply that anyone who commits an evil act is deluded in some way. This is why there are only a very few ethical principles that are held in common across nearly all societies, as we shall see later. Meanwhile, in religious societies the explanation for evil in a general sense rests with theology.

Of course, if one does not believe such a god exists then there is no problem since a combination of Free Will and "shit happens" is quite capable of explaining it. However, the Simulation Argument and the Maya it generates forces us to look anew at the question which has its origins at least as far back as ancient Greece with the philosopher Epicurus. Restated it becomes:

> "Either God wants to abolish evil, and cannot; or he can, but does not want to. ... If he wants to, but cannot, he is impotent. If he can, but does not want to, he is wicked. ... If, as they say, God can abolish evil, and God really wants to do it, why is there evil in the

world?"

In our case "God" is actually the entity presiding over one of the levels of Maya. Obviously if it is run in a hands-off fashion we have a god that is indifferent to what is happening in this universe, certainly up until this point in time, but one thing seems fairly certain is that it is not an overtly malicious, capricious or frivolous world we find ourselves in. The evil, and good, within it is pretty much all our own work. It is also lawful in that effects have causes and the world is not dominated by arbitrary and inexplicable happenings. Finally, there are no obvious Gods, or even people with superhuman powers (yet), constantly messing with reality. It is not a comic-book world. Yet even here, is there scope for some redeeming feature that might make the evil we suffer worthwhile, even when it appears completely pointless? The answer may be a qualified yes.

The noted physicist Frank Tipler, in his book *The Physics of Immortality*, addresses this question and asks how a moral entity responsible for creating this world might reconcile the hands-off approach with the pointless suffering that will inevitably result. He concludes that an answer might lie in a part of the Maya reserved as a traditional style afterlife, where all wrongs are righted. Of course, this still does not really provide an answer to the immediacy of suffering let alone why the Maya exists in the first place. However, it does suggest that things may never be as bad as they seem. In fact, if we are in a Maya designed to reconstruct us from the past then the reason for evil and personal suffering is obvious – it is the price paid by us to live again, with the further implied promise of immortality and the end of suffering as we transition to a higher state of consciousness in a world vast beyond our imagination. It is also a price we pay to try and help save those who inflict that suffering upon us.

There could be a whole hierarchy with each taking the equivalent of a computer backup of the entities within it, and each Maya collapsing in to the larger one when its computing requirements exceed a certain level. So, for example, Tipler's universe could back up that of the Progenitors, who back up that of the Gaia, who backs up the PostHumans, who back up us. One way of resolving what happens to the "dead" is to allow each level to determine what happens to its own ancestors upon transition to a higher level. For example, all the dead of our world would be made accessible to us for judgment at the point when we attain PostHuman status. This also resolves old and rather trivial theological issues concerning the implementation problems of a traditional afterlife. To illustrate, consider a person whose beloved spouse dies and who then remarries an equally loved partner. Who gets to live with who in the hereafter? The answer in this case is simple – multiple copies and multiple parallel afterlives. Additionally, we should not expect an eternal state but one where issues are resolved and the inhabitants educated as to their true condition before being advanced to the next plane of existence. For now though, let's return to the type of world we are likely to be inhabiting, Maya run by PostHuman Shen.

In a solipsistic reality the problem of evil can be resolved in a fully ethical manner. The resolution is simple – everyone here is me, and I am a volunteer. All the suffering we see about us is self inflicted. That's the easy bit. The dangerous and ethically dubious question is this: Does it matter if I inflict suffering upon myself in the form of the NPCs? Is harming someone whom I intellectually consider to have no real existence, and hence cannot feel real pain, wrong? I would suggest that the answer is a tentative "yes" if only because by our actions do we define what we are. Whenever the temptation to do evil is successfully resisted it makes us stronger, and even if we are only a character in our own dream its effect will ripple up the chain of reality to the dreaming psyche. We should bear in mind that a PostHuman Shen will likely have near total control over elements of its psyche – certainly to the extent of being able to excise undesirable tendencies when they have served their purpose, and conversely to absorb and magnify the good and beneficial. What it boils down to is the question of who we want to be, and which elements of our character we want to eliminate or strengthen. This then becomes the testing ground.

Things are more complex if this reality is a result of a collaboration of several Shen minds, because it is more likely to be generated from a shared mindspace, and where we are not the Shen themselves but their avatars. Whether there would be a real difference between a Shen "unconscious" and an avatar is however a moot point. The problem of raising NPCs to full consciousness by interacting deeply with them becomes acute. For example consider people in various Third World hell-holes; people who have by any definition, suffered and are suffering terribly. Right now, in my Maya, they are just stories in a newspaper, or pictures on a TV screen. If I were to become an aid worker, go over there and try to help, would I actually be fleshing out the Maya with NPCs and raising them to the point of consciousness where their pain would be as real as anything I could experience? In short, would I be multiplying the evil in the world simply by looking at it in detail? An interesting speculation, but we must take the world at face value and seek to mitigate or alleviate the misery we encounter in this world as much for our own sake as for others.

And since it would be a Maya shared by our peers how we treat other potentially sentient Beings becomes rather important. This is especially so if this is some kind of test. If so, what qualities are the Shen looking for? It's difficult to say, but it would seem reasonable to assume that they are not looking for serial killers, genocidal maniacs or the petty evil to uplift to a reality of comparative Godhood. Neither, in a world of computational richness, would they especially value intelligence over character.

The obvious question is what does one do with all the serial killers, mass murderers and other multitudinous undesirables that Humanity regularly throws up? It would definitely not be a good idea to give them superhuman powers and set them loose amongst the Gods. There will ultimately have to be some kind of Judgment Day where at the very least the recalcitrant are "tweaked" or wiped if after multiple opportunities they do not learn to mend their ways.

Judgment Day

In many conventional religions there is some form of Judgment Day that takes the form of you finding your postmortem self standing before the deity in order to have your past life judged or evaluated. The outcome determines whether you be consigned to Heaven and eternal life, Hell and eternal torment, oblivion or maybe reincarnation to try again. The criteria for such consignments are almost always the degree to which you have followed the rules laid down by the alleged deity, or broken them. In ancient Egypt the Goddess Ma'at weighed the heart, or conscience, on a set of scales representing balance and justice. It was weighed against a feather, which although very light was not weightless, so absolute perfection was not required to pass the test. If the heart proved heavier due to the dead not having lived according to the principles of Ma'at it was thrown into a lake of fire. If it was lighter than the feather the dead entered into eternal life.

This mythological process finally evolved to the point where the Christian God condemns everybody even before they are born due to the notion of Original Sin, requiring an intermediary (Jesus) to plead on their behalf and wash away the sins so that the spotless soul may enter into Heaven. With Islam, Allah is somewhat more merciful during the process and perfection not necessary. In the latter religions Judgment Day occurs at a specific time and not immediately after death when all the dead (and those still living) are collected or resurrected to face God. I will omit the finer points of Christian/Islamic theology and leave them as an exercise for the reader. The question, however, is this: How realistic is it to expect something like this to occur? In the universe as presented by contemporary science the answer is that it is impossible. If we are enmeshed in Maya, as seems likely, then it will be almost inevitable.

There are two ways in which we may find ourselves before the apocryphal Judgment Seat. The most obvious is by dying and then being resurrected in order to be evaluated, the other is by living through the Apocalypse. Why should any of us be brought back to life? One might hazard a guess: Because it is just, because it is the only suitable recompense for the suffering in the world, and because we deem it so. In other words, some of us who pass through the Singularity to PostHuman Godhood will carry this duty with them and fulfill it for their ancestors, friends and family who did not survive. Once more the question is asked: Who speaks for the dead?

If as seems likely there is a different kind of apocalypse manifested as an unveiling between the different levels of Maya, that is between different levels of cosmic simulation, the process is similar. The only difference is that we have already been through this, and will pass through it again. With each unveiling comes judgment because, simply stated, would you as a Godlike entity just give everyone who ever lived similar powers to yourself, or would you exercise some discretion in the matter? There is not too much of a problem when a benevolent compassionate and righteous person stands before you, but it's quite a different matter when its a borderline insane serial killer or one of the nastier characters from history. Then there is the vast bulk of Humankind who fall somewhere between the two extremes. There is a C S Lewis quote later in the book which speaks of the immortality of ordinary people and their spiritual destiny. It ends:

> "...But it is with immortals whom we joke with, work with, marry, snub, and exploit – immortal horrors or everlasting splendours."

I think we would rather prefer people who are destined to become everlasting splendors rather than immortal horrors. In fact, we might well decide we do not want any immortal horrors at all. So we can expect one of three verdicts: pass, fail, try again.

"Pass" seems fairly simple, but it is not quite as obvious as it seems since nobody is perfect. The option would be given to "wash their sins away", that is, to have the (minor) parts of their spirit/personality that are still undesirable to both the Goddess and the supplicant altered or erased so that they may be uplifted to PostHuman Shen perfection, power and immortality.

"Try Again" would be an option whereby the supplicant opts not to have their spirit modified and wants to do it themselves. In which case they are thrown back into the Maya at a suitable point in history – reincarnation. This option may arise because of a peculiarity of computer programs in general, and Human minds in particular. It turns out that there is no general way to look at a complex program and deciding what its output will be, except by running it. There are no shortcuts. It could also be that immersion in the Maya of contemporary existence *is* the judgment process as the Goddess "runs" us. It may also explain the prevalence of such imagery in all major religions – because we have been here before, and perhaps will be again. It is here we encounter a real mechanism for the evolution of souls. Whether we can recall any aspects of our previous lives is a moot point because they would almost certainly not be historically accurate simply because history as a whole would be different each incarnation. Indeed, the incarnation may well be repeatedly set in the same time period, resulting not in past lives but effectively parallel lives. Having recall of such a parallel life would be more like remembering a dream where everything is subtly wrong, or deja vu on a large scale. We might meet people we think we recognize but know that it is impossible, or experience false memories.

"Fail" would be the most terminal option. It means that whoever has this judgment passed upon them cannot have their spirit modified without it obliterating their personality. That their evil is so entwined with who they are that they cannot be separated from it, nor do they want to be. It would also mean that multiple reincarnations have failed to alter the situation and the only option left is to allow them to die for the final time and be deleted. At their last judgment they would not be present.

The judgment process itself cannot be anything but utterly fair. This is not like a Human court of law with the defendant arguing their case through their lawyers on points of law, mitigating circumstances and so forth while attempting to uncover the truth (or hide it). The Goddess knows every aspect of their past history and soul to the tiniest detail including motivations as well as their existing state of mind and spirit in perfect detail. It is not like a criminal asking the judge for mercy because they are sorry for what they did. If they are truly sorry She will know, if not She will also know. The key element of repentance is whether, given the same circumstances and a belief they will not be caught, the malefactor would commit the same crime again. This too is beyond doubt. This is not to say there will be no element of mercy, because much evil is committed by the insane or mentally unbalanced, which as we now recognize is largely a matter of the interaction of genetics and environment, or even brain damage – evil committed by the deluded out of ignorance. Different circumstances may well yield radically different outcomes, hence reincarnation. On a penultimate note, if you are still alive there is still all to win no matter what your situation.

So we return to the story of Ma'at and one last factor – conscience. It is the deciding factor when it comes to repentance in that while someone may do something wrong multiple times there is a difference between doing so out of weakness by acting against ones conscience and doing so with no conscience at all. It is a lot easier to make someone strong than make someone good.

Fate, Angels and Demons

If we are enmeshed in a form of Maya, are we the only ones? Are there likely to be non-Human intelligences around as well?

In the larger scale Maya with multiple people in the process of resurrection there must be some mechanism in place for when free will unreasonably asserts itself and things go awry. It would be increasingly difficult to erase segments of time from the Maya to enable a replay for a few individuals if it would affect everyone else. So there may be special functions whose job it is to make sure things stay on track – agents or avatars of Gaia. In other words, angels. However, it is extremely unlikely they would manifest in an apparently supernatural form. Rather, they would work through ordinary people, guiding their consciousness and choices in subtle way to steer others onto the desired path, or away from spiritual harm. This does not mean "saving lives" or even helping in a conventional sense since in this situation a life is not the most important issue. It means saving souls, and they would "move in mysterious ways", perhaps occasionally using people who consciously opened themselves for that purpose. On the other hand, there may be people here who are old souls and who have chosen to continue here rather than graduate to the next level in order to help others to pass the inevitable testing. Buddhists have a name for them as well – Bodhisattvas. Almost all religions have this "Holy Stranger" mythic archetype, where they are either a God, or messenger of the Gods, who come to earth in disguise to either carry out orders from above or just perform good deeds. It may well be that the disguise is so good that they themselves do not know who they are!

As to what kind of jobs they do, it might range from the seemingly insignificant – a word or even glance that changes the course of someones actions at a critical part of their lives, to the very large scale. For example, it seems miraculous that for nearly half a century the world stood on the edge of the abyss of global nuclear war, with two armed camps and tens of thousands of nuclear weapons awaiting immediate launch. Yet despite some extremely close calls, this never happened and the situation resolved relatively peacefully. If anyone is looking for divine intervention, that would be a good place to start.

The Demonic Worlds

So far we have not delved too deeply into the possibility of there being worlds or beings that are actively hostile to us, partly because we do not overtly live in such a world. Yet as Humanity passes through the Singularity there are bound to be individuals who are at least amoral agents and who will gain demigod status along with the rest. This is of course making the very reasonable assumption that Humanity as a whole will not have sorted out our problems with the criminals and psychopaths before this happens, especially since there seems to be a disproportionate number running the world at present.

Similarly there are bound to be artificial intelligences that are by no means ideal from our point of view. One only has to think of the military and future weapons systems. They will certainly not be hampered by compassion or notions of universal love. Just the opposite, which is why it is important to try and limit these devices in any way we can. The only hope is that they are kept in check to a large degree by those around them who have similar powers. Beyond that, not much can or should be said.

So, looking at the factors upon which we will be judged brings us to the ethics of the Praxis and that C S Lewis quote.

Ethics

"It is a serious thing to live in a society of possible gods and goddesses, to remember that the dullest and most uninteresting person you can talk to may one day be a creature which, if you saw it now, you would be strongly tempted to worship, or else a horror and a corruption such as you now meet, if at all, only in a nightmare. All day long we are, in some degree helping each other to one or other of these destinations. It is in the light of these overwhelming possibilities, it is with the awe and the circumspection proper to them, that we should conduct all our dealings with one another, all friendships, all loves, all play, all politics. There are no ordinary people. You have never met a mere mortal. Nations, cultures, arts, civilizations – these are mortal, and their life is to ours as the life of a gnat. But it is with immortals whom we joke with, work with, marry, snub, and exploit – immortal horrors or everlasting splendors." C S Lewis, *Weight of Glory*

Ironically Lewis was speaking of what he considered to be the immortal soul in a Christian context. However, it certainly applies to all that has gone before, and herein lies the core of our ethics – that one day we all may have the powers of Gods, for good or evil. Furthermore, that our interactions and dealings with each other shape the kind of people they (and we) ultimately become.

However, there are only a few really universal ethical principles that it would be wise to observe without reservation.

The Oath

In our ethical structure there is really very little that is prescriptive. We have no commandments written in stone but we do have a the notion of honorable behavior. At the heart of this concept lies the ideal of keeping ones word - The Oath.

To clarify further, an Oath is a formal declaration of truth or a promise made by an individual – a declaration of what was, is, or will be. The most common examples of the formal Oath are to be found in the wedding vows, Oaths given in a court of law and oaths of allegiance and service when embarking upon a career in the police or military. Within the Praxis, as within legal frameworks, it is important to note that it is the detail of the wording, and the specified actions and obligations that matter. One is held to account by deeds, rather than unspecified intentions.

There are only a few legitimate ways to be free from the obligations of an Oath. They are:

> To be released from it by whomever or whatever it was made to or before
> To be released from it by circumstances that have rendered it meaningless
> To be released from it by a failure upon the part of another who is party to it
> To be released from it by completing the obligations of the Oath

The reason it is so central is that of all positions it is the one that is not susceptible to a relativist interpretation. It is a core of morality that every people, every civilization past, present and future must acknowledge as absolute because it is measured and judged ultimately not by people or even Gods, but by consensus reality - the reality that lies within the domain of experimental proof – science. Simply stated, by taking an Oath we are aligning our innermost self with the reality of the words we speak. In spiritual terms we are "putting our soul where our mouth is". Or, in more prosaic terms, we are putting our psychological integrity on the line.

If the Oath is in the form of a promise, it has "magickal" properties – it creates Reality in accordance with Will. So, why should we take an Oath seriously? What are the penalties for breaking one? From a social contract point of view the penalties range from nothing, through loss of trustworthiness, loss of "face" and up to execution depending upon the specific Oath and its legal jurisdiction.

To return to the beginning, why do we take an Oath in the first place? It is to define our exact position in the spiritual and material realm, either to ourselves, to society, or to our Deities. It is a declaration of who we are, defined by where we stand, or where we will be. A major consequence of this is that an Oath localizes us in the psycho-physical, almost as if it were a mapping co-ordinate laid upon an apparently chaotic realm. As a result, no matter what follows, the Oath changes our access to, and view of, that landscape. It is a permanent mark. So, what happens when it is broken is that we are no longer aligned by the Reality we define for ourselves – there arises a dissonance and we become lost as the map we have drawn becomes worthless.

As we have seen previously, our minds and our notions of self are actually not unitary things, but are composites made up of many facets that ideally work in harmony. Breaking an Oath is a major step onto the downward path by creating an instant division in ourselves that is effectively permanent as long as the memory and reality clash. Of course, if an Oath breaker starts in that state and the Oath means nothing to begin with, then they are not going to be worse off. They may, in fact, profit in the short term from such a deception. It is a strategy for the weak - those who lack a morality. It also means that they are chronically unable to define themselves in the world as anything but a grab bag of uncontrolled desires and cravings responding in an expedient short-term manner. They have no focus in the spiritual realm, but are diffuse objects lost in what seems like a hostile environment. Once again, a description of them in everyday speech would be that they "have no presence of mind". They are not capable of acting in a coherent, effective way in the world, and are certainly incapable of any magickal practices. Like most generalizations, there are interesting exceptions.

Many religions have specialized in saving one from such a predicament, that is, in offering "Salvation". There are two methods that I am aware of that could be effective after the fact. They both amount to essentially the same thing, and are exceptionally difficult (and hence unlikely, despite what practitioners may claim). It is "Being Reborn", which means changing to such an extent that there is no direct causal (Karmic) link between the old and new. Christianity allegedly does so by replacing the old Mind with a new, God centered, one. Buddhism does it by quieting the Mind to such an extent that the Ocean stops churning, and there is so little remaining in the way of turbulence that any divisions that once existed have negligible effects. The extinguishing of desire – the putting out of the fire – the cooling after a fever – Nirvana.

In essence, these methods reflect a difference in spirituality between East and West.

The notion of "attachment" also arises, not only in terms of the Oath, but also in terms of general mental health. With Buddhism, the aim is non-attachment. It means that we do not invest anything of ourselves in the world of Illusion or Ideas or Concepts etc. The rationale is that all composite things are transitory, hence impermanent. By attaching to things that will cease to exist (or maybe existed only as projected figments of the imagination) we are chaining ourselves to a sinking ship. When that ship sinks, it tears part of the Mind. I have experienced that feeling upon the death of a friend – the part of me that was attached to her felt like it had been torn away and had left a gaping hole, and I was incomplete. Perhaps one of the reasons for a naive belief in the afterlife is to prevent such wounds and sense of loss from causing a permanent disfigurement of the mental landscape. Anyway, to return to the notion of attachment in the Praxis I would maintain that we do not withdraw from the world, as Buddhism has a tendency to do. We take a more pragmatic approach. Namely, we should attach as far as possible only to the atemporal - to Principles. Buddhism at its ultimate does not even attach to the idea of non-attachment, or to Being or Non Being! The point being, if one were totally non attached to the Oath, or its requirements, or benefits or consequences one might take it and/or break it at will without Karmic consequence, although one does wonder what motivations might be for doing so, or how such may arise at all. Non attachment allows one to move through the world without causing much in the way of ripples. It is the essence of invisibility.

Finally, the analysis of the Oath also applies to a lesser extent to the notions of telling truth and lies, and while the effects are generally lesser, chronic dishonesty makes up for in quantity what it lacks in quality.

The Golden Rule

Simply stated: Treat others as you wish to be treated yourself. Or, conversely, do not treat others in a way that you do not wish to be treated yourself.

This has implications that go far beyond simply acting as a guide for how we treat other people. At one end of the spectrum are animals and the natural world, and at the other the godlike machines and entities that we will eventually create, or become. That alters the traditional perspective of Humanity being top of the ethical chain and therefore uniquely in a position to determine the worth of all other life, since to our successors *we* will be no more to them than animals are to us. From an ethical point of view how we treat those who are totally in our power is a measure of our moral worth. Right now Humanity as a whole is not doing too well on that front, even within our own species. No doubt when we are totally at the mercy of a higher power we would prefer that it take a rather more benevolent approach to us than we do to animals. Indeed, it might be a matter of survival that we do not set the ugly precedent of "Might makes Right" if we get around to creating superhuman intelligence at any point. Maybe it will learn by example. So perhaps an updated variation of the Golden Rule would be simply to treat other lifeforms as we would wish a God to treat us.

This also leads to the updated Biblical injunction of Mathew 1:7 "Judge not lest you be judged". Despite what many people believe, this is not a prohibition on making judgments but that those who make a judgment will be held to the same standards by a higher power. The latter can be variously defined. In our context two interpretations apply. The first is that of material reality. If, for example, I judge that I can jump across a gap and not fall I will be judged by reality. The penalty for making a false judgment being proportional to ambition, daring and of course failure. The second is the spiritual interpretation where a judgment is made that has implications for the well-being of another person. Here the higher power is the entity dreaming this reality, and making such a judgment is tantamount to us volunteering to be held to the same standards. Again, this seems obvious, but what if the criteria we use are blatantly unfair? Are we asking God to be equally unfair to us in return? If so, I hope that God does not listen and in its position of superior knowledge and wisdom shows compassion, but we should be looking over our collective shoulder and consider the possibility that we may ultimately be held accountable by our own creations. Finally, if we do not want to be held to our own standards, but still apply them to other people that is straightforward hypocrisy – a black mark against one's own soul due to the inconsistency.

Compassion

This is another critical feature of our ethics. Compassion has been defined as the active desire to alleviate suffering. It is more rigorous than empathy in that it embodies the notion of an imperative to action. While empathy is a feeling, compassion seeks to make changes in the world. As such it is a cornerstone of all the great religions and ethical philosophies. It is also something we should attempt to cultivate not only in ourselves and our

Human institutions but when we are able we should seek to instil it in created intelligence. The last thing we want is for our Artilect Gods to treat us as we treat animals. Or, if they do, then it would be far better for us to have the status of beloved pets rather than farm animals, lab rats or simply vermin. One might also hope that we can infuse them with such notions as gratitude, duty and the payment of moral debts, most notably to us for bringing them into existence.

The Praxis

The understanding of humanity will be the death of humanity.
And give way for the birth of angels,
who fear not the loss of meaning.
For through the noosphere,
the universe will pour into them
an overwhelming gratitude
of the great tree of life,
its eons of groping in the dark,
suffering ignorantly, innumerable deaths
with their hearts of hidden despair,
and upon which its painful awakening,
blooming into the divine light,
will finally give birth to them.

The Death of Illusory Love and the Ascension of Being – Jamie Dunbaugh

A question that is often not addressed in Transhumanism when the subject of reviving the dead into some form of fulfilling life arises, is this: who will care enough to do it? After all, the dead are not going to complain. Indeed, with cryonics there may well be material incentives *not* to revive them. Scattered throughout this book the question is phrased:

"Who will speak for the dead".

One answer is family. I would certainly resurrect my parents, grandparents and those friends of mine who have died. In turn, I would hope that my (step) children and friends would do it for me in turn. The problem is that maybe the technology to do all this lies far enough in the future that family duty or emotional bond will have weakened to the point where they are ineffective. For example, I do not even know who my great grandparents really were – they are just names in a book, probably dead before I was born. That leaves either the benevolence of strangers or some sort of organization who would provide this service. So, what sort of organizations might be capable of surviving the Singularity and the turmoil associated with it, and would be prepared to look after their deceased members interests as family would? Only two spring to mind – large scale organized religion and its secular counterpart Freemasonry.

Certainly nothing as transitory as governments, nations or businesses. The Roman Catholic Church is the prime example in that it has survived and prospered for nearly two thousand years, longer than most contemporary nations have existed, and it will doubtless survive in some form after most have faded into history. We must attempt to comprise the third, and be far more focused than any others on our transcendent duty. Hopefully for a far shorter time until our mission is completed.

There is one more point that should be borne in mind concerning family, and children in particular. The founder of Zero State, Amon Kalkin, was recently asked by an American woman whether Transhumanism supported "family values". Now, for those who do not know, this is a politically loaded term for all kinds of conservative ideology. Nevertheless, a literal answer can be given: Yes, we support family values in the widest possible sense. We are fully inclusive and this especially means families and children. Finally a note on parenting that is a bad taste joke that might not be a joke - be kind to your children and bring them up well, or you risk staying dead.

Immanentizing the Eschaton

In political theory and theology, to immanentize the Eschaton means trying to bring about the Eschaton, the final heaven-like stage of history, in the immanent world. Immanence, derived from the Latin "in-manere" meaning "to remain within", refers to philosophical and metaphysical theories of divine presence, in which the divine is seen to be manifested in or encompassing of the material world. It is this that the Praxis explicitly seeks, and moreover, seeks to pass beyond. While conventionally the Eschaton is "the end of days" for us it is a transformational point signaling a new dawn – the real beginning of history as we move out of these dark ages of stupidity, cruelty and ignorance. Hence we advocate and support individual routes to transcendence. The only thing we need to take with us into the light of the new world is our spirit and our purpose.

Organization of the Praxis

Those who wish to adopt the aims of the Praxis and live a lifestyle in accordance with it are to be known as the Consensus. The formal grouping of members of the Consensus are to known as Domains. These concepts correspond to congregations and churches, or if Freemasonry is the analogy, the fraternity/sorority and Lodge.

The domain structure requires a minimum of three people as members comprising the initial Triumvirate, which is the ruling body. Unless the domain is single gender only the Triumvirate must always comprise at least one male and one female. Normally after a minimum of one year and a maximum of five there would be elections for the position on the triumvirate. Each member of the triumvirate (Triumvir) would have different responsibilities, typically administration, social event planning and education. Any member of the triumvirate may officiate at ceremonial events as the Magister, or master of ceremonies. A Domain is explicitly an organization intended to include whole families in its social events.

However, a minimum age is specified for full membership of the Praxis, and that is twenty one years. None under this age may take the required Oaths. They may however be registered as Candidates, which entitles them to participate in activities of their home Domain at the discretion of the Consensus, but no others.

It is envisaged that there may be specialist Domains dedicated to particular aspects of spirituality or other endeavors. These are referred to as *Synods*, meaning "A council or an assembly" usually of church officials or churches, and can be color coded:

- Red Synod – single gender
- Yellow Synod – philosophy
- Green Synod – polytheist
- Blue Synod – monotheist
- Violet Synod – atheist
- White Synod – all welcome
- Black Synod – esoteric spirituality

Alternatively, one could append the color to special interest groups within, or between, Domains. It should be noted that these synods are intended to be minority activities and most Domains should be White.

Sacraments

A Sacrament has been variously defined as:

- A rite in which a God or Goddess is uniquely active
- A visible symbol of an invisible reality
- An outward and visible sign of an inner invisible grace

A sacrament confers variously: forgiveness of sins, conveys the divine grace and blessing of the God or Goddess, sanctity or holiness and indicates membership of the Church. Of course, these are originally Christian concepts but they form one of the key elements of what a religion "does", and how it defines and binds it membership.

The choice of sacraments by a given Domain will be up to the membership and largely defined by the Synod to which it belongs. The following descriptions are not exhaustive, but illustrative. Some are obviously unsuitable for minors and hence not "family friendly". In general, they fall into several broad categories, which may overlap. There are:

- Sacraments of Mind – Intellectual
  Which includes the teaching and practice of prayer and meditation techniques, learning and practice of NLP and hypnotic techniques, development of ritual and theater
- Sacraments of Body – Physical
  Dance, martial arts, tantric sex, feasting and fasting
- Sacraments of Spirit – The subconscious mind
  The use of entheogens, mind altering technologies such as sensory deprivation, sleep deprivation, drumming, chanting
- Sacraments of Community – Social
  Charity work, proselytizing, networking, self help, publicly advocating and defending the search for transcendence, parties and generally having fun

Rites and Rituals

Rites and rituals are used in almost all religions and fraternities to bind the group together spiritually for common purpose. They do so by creating a feeling of belonging as well as reminding or teaching the members of their purpose in gathering together and the reason for the existence of the organization. They facilitate easy movement of members between disparate parts of the organization that may be separated geographically by providing the basis of a common culture. In the case of the Roman Catholic Church until recently this also involved using Latin as a common international language.

The variety of observances covers all the major events in Human life from birth, initiation into the organization, through to marriage and finally funeral and remembrance services for the dead. Interspersed are regular meetings, feasts and celebrations and of course Holy Days (holidays). There may also be special courses to educate the membership in the theology or ideology at varying intervals.

What follows is intended to be a bare outline of such ceremonies to be undertaken. It is envisaged that there will be an organic evolution of such practices by the various groups as they see fit and adapt them to the local culture. What is laid down here should be incorporated and built upon but is far from the final word on the matter. The core element of each ritual is a reminder and acknowledgment of the nature of reality and the intent of the Praxis, reinforced with a sense of participation of the guests and/or Consensus via a call and response format. This is one very common method of structuring a ceremony designed for participation of a large number of people, not all of whom are familiar with what is happening. The priest, or whoever is leading, makes a brief statement to which the congregation either intones a ritual affirmation, simply repeats the statement, or repeats the last words of the statement, as directed.

The final note concerning rites and rituals involves clothing, traditionally a very important part of the theater associated with the proceedings. This is completely optional, varying from none at all to normal everyday clothes to robes and vestments. Each Domain will choose their regalia and jewelery, if any, and upon which occasions it should be worn. The only commonality is to be the use of the Greek letter Phi to signify the Praxis as a whole. In mathematics it is commonly used to denote the Golden Ratio. The symbol maybe be used in either a plain or a stylized fashion, alone or in conjunction with other symbolism.

Initiation into a Domain of the Praxis

The candidate must be publicly sponsored by two full members of the Domain who will attest to his or her good character, and should have attended at least one social function. Additionally, the candidate must be instructed as to the nature of the Praxis, its beliefs, benefits and duties, and the Oaths that they will be asked to swear. Any objection to the candidate becoming a member must be made by an existing member and be presented in writing to the Triumvirate for consideration. The candidate, objector and sponsors will present their case before the Triumvirate who will then make a decision as to whether to proceed with the initiation. The decision is binding, but only in that particular Domain.

The setting for the initiation is a meeting attended by at least two of the three members of the Triumvirate. Other members of the Domain are allowed, and indeed encouraged, to attend the investiture. Note that some of these Oaths are matters of individual interpretation and conscience, and others are not.

The candidate is introduced to the assembly by the Magister, flanked by the sponsors.

Magister: *State your name*

Candidate: *My name is [name]*

Magister: *Do your sponsors vouch for your good character?*

Sponsors: *I do*

Magister: *Do you understand the solemn and binding nature of the vows you are about to undertake, and enter into them of your own free will knowing that they will be written upon your soul before Gods and mortals?*

Candidate: *I do*

Magister: *Know then that the purpose of our fellowship is to seek eternal life and reunion with those who have passed before us. To seek knowledge and perfection of spirit and soul that we may become worthy to resurrect the willing* dead and in turn be judged worthy to journey into the worlds beyond. Such powers may lie in our past or in our future. Meanwhile we shall remember those who have passed and we shall speak for them as family so that come the Awakening none will be forgotten. We shall be the calm in the storm, the eye of the hurricane, the refuge in the night, the hope for tomorrow. Now speak your Oaths.

Magister: *First, the Oath of Initiation into the Praxis. Candidate, repeat after me – I swear...*

That if it is in my power to do so... I will resurrect the willing dead... and allow them to progress to the destinations they sought or hoped for in life... Having done so... I will reveal the truth of their situation... and offer whatever resources are necessary and possible to complete their journey... in the light of the new reality... consistent with the well-being of other sentient creatures.

Magister: *Now, the Oaths of the Praxis. Candidate, repeat after me - I swear...*

All my dealing with my brothers and sisters of the Praxis shall be honest and fair

All my words and speech with my brothers and sisters of the Praxis shall be considered and polite

All my debts, whether material or spiritual, to my brothers and sisters of the Praxis shall be repaid

I shall aid my brothers and sisters of the Praxis in any way I can and as I see fit providing it is ethical to do so

I shall favor my brothers and sisters of the Praxis above all others and in all things, if all else be equal

I shall strive to bring renown and glory to my own name and the Praxis through good deeds and spiritual progress for all my life

Magister: *You are no longer a candidate, but a Fellow of this Domain of the Praxis. Live by your words spoken here today, for they are eternally binding.*

> *Welcome [brother/sister] and enjoy the rights, responsibilities and benefits to which you have bound yourself. May you find that which you seek even though the path be long and difficult. Know now that you are not alone.*

Formal Ceremonies and Meetings

These are generally social and educational events and will be opened with the words:

> **Magister**: *Know then that the purpose of our fellowship is to seek eternal life and reunion with those who have passed before us. To seek knowledge and perfection of spirit and soul that we may become worthy to resurrect the willing dead and in turn be judged worthy to be resurrected into the worlds beyond. Such powers may lie in our past or in our future. Meanwhile we shall remember those who have passed and we shall speak for them as family so that come the Awakening none will be forgotten. We shall be the calm in the storm, the eye of the hurricane, the refuge in the night, the hope for tomorrow.*

There are a minimum of two formal ceremonies which may be performed on Holy days (solstice and equinox). The primary one is the *Ceremony of Remembrance* and involves groups of up to approximately thirteen members standing or sitting in a circle. A Copper, Silver or wooden bowl or chalice is filled with an alcoholic drink, for example mead, wine or spirits or alternatively pure water. This is passed around the circle three times for toasts, the focus being past, present and future. When an alcoholic drink is used those who cannot or should not ingest alcohol may simply touch the bowl to their lips without drinking.

During the first round each communicant names those who have passed from this world and who are to be remembered at this time, be it family or friends. The communicant says something about each of them and why they should be returned to life. They then "drink their words" before passing on the bowl.

The second round concerns the present, where each communicant toasts those present, their brothers and sisters of the Praxis and their Domain. They may also speak briefly of issues of contemporary interest to themselves.

The final round is the future and a toast to the Gods, whether they are that which we will create, that which we will become, that which we are already are, or the impersonal forces by which we are made manifest in this world.

The second type of formal ceremony is more extended and is based upon the old Germanic pagan tradition of the Sumbl. It is designed for a small gathering in intimate surroundings where the first three rounds of cup passing are as before. However, the cup is refilled and passed again for "Oaths, boasts and toasts" and short speeches. That is, celebrants make boasts of their own deeds and accomplishments and promises of future actions. In Western culture it is generally considered bad manners to "boast", which is defined as *"to talk with excessive pride and self-satisfaction about one's achievements, possessions, or abilities"*. However, in our context we can omit the "excessive" and allow a modicum of pride. After all, humility is not something in which we should indulge to excess either.

This continues until all have had enough, or until a set number of rounds have elapsed. Words spoken during the Sumbl are considered and consecrated, becoming part of the destiny of those assembled. The Romans had a saying – in vino veritas: In wine, truth. Food may then follow depending upon the occasion. One permitted variation would be to replace the alcohol with some other intoxicant, but that is left to the discretion of the Domain and celebrants in the light of whatever laws may locally govern such things. The purpose is to expose the true nature of each person who partakes, and bind the whole into a unity of understanding and (hopefully) trust.

The ceremonies and rituals which now follow are optional for each Domain, but mark important stages in the lives of all and are strongly recommended.

Birth and Naming

The biggest event in life, being born and entering into the family with a naming ceremony, is one surrounded with ritual in every culture. Of particular importance is the names given to the child as regarding the reasons they are chosen and their meanings. The contemporary trend to pick names simply because they are fashionable is to be deplored. Names have meanings, and the power to shape the character of those bearing them. They should be chosen either with these meanings in mind as a gift of hoped for qualities or alternatively in honor of someone for their admirable deeds.

Suggested format and wording, delivered by the Magister:

[The child is presented to the attendees of the ceremony]

"Before friends, family, and members of the Praxis we give this child of the **[family name]** *family the name(s)* **[insert given names]**.

The names have been chosen for these reasons and have these meanings: **[names, reason for the names, meanings]**.

We welcome **[full names of child]** *into this world, a unique Being in this universe, as the new life from which his/her soul will grow into the Tree of Eternal Life. We pray that his/her life in this world, amongst those who are here today, is long, happy and successful.*

Do each of you gathered here pledge to aid **[full names of child]** *to the best of your ability to grow into a soul of honor, bravery, compassion, honesty and knowledge? To become a tribute to this world and others beyond?"*

[Each of those gathered replies to this question. The ceremony ends with the words...]

"So be it"

Marriage

The Praxis does not specify who, or what, may marry whom. Marriage is viewed by the Praxis as a close alliance of two or more individuals born out of love and as a suitable setting for the raising of children. If children are involved then it is expected that the marriage will not be dissolved before those children who are born into it become adults.

As I write, a contentious political and religious issue is raging in the UK and USA – same sex marriage. This is actually a multifaceted argument due to the fact that marriage is a religious, secular and State regulated institution affecting the legal status (or lack of it) of those being married (or not). Through "official" marriage the state implements a wide ranging and binding contract upon those being married with respect to property and inheritance rights, amongst others. This without even getting into issues of polygamy, polyandry and polyamory.

In line with Zero State policy the Praxis is going to ignore the impact of national laws upon marriage and consider it purely from a spiritual and contract point of view. So, there are two aspects. The first concerns the legal consequences. It is expected that the celebrants know the de facto legal situation to which the ceremony binds them if it is also state sanctioned. Where it is not, or in addition, the celebrants should consider a legal contract explicitly stating their wishes in the event of dissolution of the marriage by consent, or by death in this world. Also in line with Praxis ethics, Oaths taken are serious matters – so be very careful what promises are made.

Finally, whether a Domain places constraints upon the parties who wish to marry depends purely upon the nature of the Domain. For example, same sex marriage may or may not be permitted, depending upon Synod orientation.

Suggested format and wording, delivered by the Magister:

[Friends and family are gathered together]

> *Magister: "We are gathered here today to join [**name**] and [**name**] in Holy Matrimony, to become as one in mind, body and spirit from this day forward, to comfort and aid each other in good times and bad, to intertwine souls in the branches of the Tree of Life and ultimately to save each other when the time comes to speak for the dead.*
>
> *Do you [**name**] accept these joys and responsibilities and pledge your loyalty to [**name**] before friends and family, Gods and mortals?*
>
> Celebrant: *"I do"*
>
> *Do you [**name**] accept these joys and responsibilities and pledge your loyalty to [**name**] before Gods and mortals?*

Celebrant: *"I do"*

Magister: *"If you have other statements you wish to make or Oaths to take you may do so now"*

[The celebrants speak, and rings may be exchanged]

Magister: *"You are now married in the eyes of the Praxis – we wish you prosperity, health, happiness and long life together in this world. Let the celebrations begin."*

Funeral Rites

The final event for the body of a person in this universe is death, and if no comprehensive preservation strategy such as cryonics is implemented, then the end point is dissolution into the environment. These rites center around the reminder that we are immortal, and that those who remain behind in this world need not permanently lose their loved ones. Death is an illusion.

The disposition of the body, unless deliberately preserved with resurrection in mind, is not a matter that concerns the Praxis. However, it is assumed that there will be a funeral or remembrance ceremony.

This is a very brief recommended format since we really do believe that we are immortal and will live again to be reunited with our loved ones in a world made perfect. However, it should be borne in mind that such rites are for the living and not the dead. Especially they are for the living who are not members of the Praxis and who perhaps see death as a permanent loss, and not a temporary parting. It is to them that whatever words of comfort and aid should be directed by the Magister.

Suggested minimal format and wording, delivered by the Magister:

[Friends and family are gathered together]

*"We are gathered here today to mourn the passing of [**name**] from this world as s/he continues onwards towards the Awakening into eternal life. While*

s/he has departed our world, we have not departed his/hers and we will remember.

In time, if we wish it, we shall meet again in a world made right where all tears will be washed away, all sins resolved, and love reigns in perfect knowledge. This is the pledge of the Consensus of the Praxis.

Who here speaks for the dead?"

> **[Each of those gathered replies to this question]**

"I speak for the dead"

The End

But how could you live and have no story to tell?
Fyodor Dostoyevsky (White Nights)

Something that has always fascinated me about religions is how the believers define themselves. Precisely, what is it that defines (say) a Christian or a Muslim? Especially given the fact that they have historically tended to kill each other, and their own coreligionists, over fine points of theology. Anyway, I will not speak for them but I can discuss the minimum you have to do, say or believe in order to call yourself a member of the Praxis.

Belief is the simple bit. You do not have to believe anything. What you should agree to do is look upon *some* of the ideas in this book as being possible and take an open minded approach to them. Specifically, the notion that we can at some future date take the Transhumanist project to completion by whatever means, and create machines or evolve into people who are far smarter, healthier, long lived, compassionate and spiritual than exist at present and who will undoubtedly have far greater insights into the nature of reality than we do. And that we/they may indeed have the ability to revive the dead of ages past.

As for *doing* there is only one promise to make and keep, which is the Oath of Initiation. Also mandatory is the minimal ethics of the Praxis, which are hardly onerous and generally boil down to being consistent, seeking to improve oneself at all times and being a goodhearted person willing to help others. That is, being a decent Human Being.

When it comes to *saying* – you can tell people about this or you can keep it to yourself. It's up to you.

Also, nobody anywhere ever gets to use the beliefs of the Praxis as justification to persecute or kill any sentient creature. If they try to do so they are automatically non-members of the Praxis. So, no crusades, jihads, inquisitions, or Holy Wars can be justified in its name. The Praxis does not need defending through either violence or censorship. As such it is morally superior to those belief systems that do.

Nothing is irrevocable, no sin is unforgivable in the eyes of the Goddess.

Finally, what if all these guesses, speculations, extrapolations and hopes are all just wishful thinking, and that none of it is real? If so, let us strive to make them real for those who follow us, and let us have fun and find good companions on the journey. If we lose we will never know it, and if we win, we win on a cosmic scale. What's the alternative – a boring life with no purpose or meaning?

What do I want?

A Life
An adventure
Great love to win and to give
Lies to unmask and truth to unveil
A place to earn at the table of the Gods
Good and trusty comrades in a hard fight
Strength tested and not found wanting
Victory against impossible odds
Evil defeated and the peace won
A life worthy of life
Transcendence
Completion

"Let a hundred flowers blossom and a hundred schools of heresy contend..."

Join with us.

www.ingramcontent.com/pod-product-compliance
Lightning Source LLC
Chambersburg PA
CBHW020012050426
42450CB00005B/440